The Joy-Full Entrepreneur:
Solutions, Signs, and Wonders

The JOY-FULL ENTREPRENEUR

Solutions, Signs & Wonders

Insider Secrets on Supernatural Business Scaling Tactics

TAMRA ANDRESS

NEW YORK

LONDON • NASHVILLE • MELBOURNE • VANCOUVER

The Joy-Full Entrepreneur: Solutions, Signs, and Wonders

Insider Secrets on Supernatural Business Scaling Tactics

Published in New York, New York by F.I.T. in Faith Press, an Imprint of Morgan James Publishing. Morgan James is a trademark of Morgan James, LLC.

www.MorganJamesPublishing.com

Proudly distributed by Publishers Group West®

A **FREE** ebook edition is available for you
or a friend with the purchase of this print book.

CLEARLY SIGN YOUR NAME ABOVE

Instructions to claim your free ebook edition:
1. Visit MorganJamesBOGO.com
2. Sign your name CLEARLY in the space above
3. Complete the form and submit a photo of this entire page
4. You or your friend can download the ebook to your preferred device

ISBN 9781636982946 paperback
ISBN 9781636982953 ebook
Library of Congress Control Number: 2023944221

Cover and Interior Design by:
Chris Treccani
www.3dogcreative.net

Edited by:
Sharon Miles Frese

A portion of all book sales goes to support The Founder Collective, a non-profit serving as a mobilzed church to establish, disciple and catalyze marketplace ministers.

*For all the entrepreneurs out there looking
to find, keep, and spread the joy.*

Table of Contents

Table of Contents (Part 2)

Per question, as answered by each contributing author

- What wisdom or encouragement would you give someone who has never blended their **faith and business strategy** as one? How has it aided in your profitability? 39, 54, 68, 79, 105, 117, 129, 154

Acknowledgments

This book would not have been possible without the individualized voices that came together to create a symphony of words representing the beauty and wonder of our Father in heaven. The hours spent laboring over your words pale in comparison to the trails you've blazed, the trials you've overcome, and the triumphs you train around in these pages.

To our contributing authors, may God's favor pour out over your business-ministries, your communities, your homes, and your hearts. May these curated chapters be representations of radiance for the time you have spent with Him and may they illuminate the lives of every person who reads in eagerness for their own solutions, signs, and wonders to be revealed.

As a publishing house, F.I.T. in Faith Press is honored to walk out the becoming process of your author journey and partner in how you testify the Good News.

We would be remiss not to recognize the incredible team behind this endeavor. The labor of love was connected to our incredible editor, Sharon Miles Frese, our content manager, Janis Rodgers, and our CFO, Candice Brown. Thank you for your endless hours and attention to detail. No one knows more intimately what it's like to work with a bunch of visionaries. Your patience and communication skills have been resourceful, and this project is excellent because of how you show up to serve.

Introduction

A lost practice in the marketplace is joy.

The American Dream has turned our jobs into a seemingly ball-and-chain requirement to exist, to establish, to maintain, and to have worth as a human. We can be caught seeking our identity in our roles and achievements, even when our initial intention was to help and serve. The weariness of the roles can weaken our heart posture and activation and also strip away one of the fundamental fruits of our labor—JOY.

We know it is not by works that we receive our identity or salvation in God, and yet the social and financial hierarchical structure of society has warped our reality of value and the truth of what we want vs. need. Consumerism, rather than consecration, has engulfed us. Consecration is the act of committing ourselves to the Lord and operating in His will; this practice asks us to release and to give rather than to take and to get. Instead of desiring to acquire, we would desire to release, which is counterculture to the conversations at large across all industries in media, education, politics, business, etc. Therefore, instead of operating out of a place of rest, we are running so hard to an invisible finish line week by week, month by month, and year by year ... anticipating a moment, a weekend, a vacation, or a season of rest that never actually comes and never instills what we actually need; Him.

Burnout, adrenal-fatigue, anxiety, depression, and the mental health crisis are all layered outcomes of the many conversations that can stem from here and have led to shifts in the way people are perceiving "work". Some would consider the shutdown of 2020 to be a forced-quit in the economy. And although the COVID-19 crisis did propel the Great Resignation, with over forty-seven million exits from the marketplace, this was only the continuation of a trend that had spanned over a decade (as reported in a Harvard Business Review). This exodus from the marketplace was also called The Great Upgrade by the deputy director of the National Economic Council because, while retirement did increase, the mass population did not stop working. Instead, they reconfigured and readjusted their work-life relationships, their priorities, their attachment to a physical location for their place of work, and their overall worth for wage needs. People aren't just tired of the hustle and grind, there are many more factors at play. Ultimately, I believe God's voice is becoming more pronounced than ever, even in day-to-day conversations that are asking bigger questions, probing new arguments, and helping people wake-up and get off the rat-wheel that has been created and sold to them as their only option for survival in the continued escalation that we live in.

Entrepreneurship boomed as a result of these scenarios and trends, spurred on by a desperation to survive and the longing to turn a "new page" (that's actually a very old page) in the book of economic cycles and the reestablishment of family values. *Business insider* reported that over five million new businesses were established in 2022, which was the second highest ever documented. Parallel to this entrepreneurial activation is the vital conversation that has resurfaced beyond the four walls of the church and into the marketplace—that of purpose and calling.

As Christ followers, we have eyes to see and ears to hear that this open door in conversation sparks opportunity for us as marketplace ministers to serve beyond people's limiting beliefs, fears, stressors, and burdens and pour into their heart's desire for more. People are seeking what Joy-full Entrepreneurs already possess—love, joy, peace—the fruit that can only be borne out of abiding rather than striving (Galatians 5:22). "Abide in Me, and I in you. As the branch cannot bear fruit of itself unless it abides in the vine, so neither can you unless you abide in Me" (John 15:4, NKJV). Jesus was a Joy-full Entrepreneur. He went about His Father's work … even as a carpenter while standing in His anointing and sharpening His knowledge, wisdom, and communication skills in the marketplace. It was then that He laid the foundation for His ministerial journey—not only in the homes and streets but in the educational and political infrastructures of that day.

The Joy-Full Entrepreneur Anthology is a project initiated to grace the bookshelves of entrepreneurs looking to realign and focus their efforts not on their works but by the grace that fuels them. Its intention isn't to just be another unread business book on the shelf of the founder, innovator, or trailblazer but to be a constant resource and reminder of who deserves our attention, who provides the manna and resources to sustain us, and the ultimate awareness of who has predestined us for good works.

This series and compilation goes beyond traditional business literature. It is a collection of personal stories, practical insights, and fresh perspectives that aim to empower Christian entrepreneurs in building the kingdom while finding joy and fulfillment in their professional lives and equipping them to become marketplace ministers. Regardless of how your faith is displayed in your brand, your business language, website copy, social media bios, or posts; your fruit is the evidence of who, how, and what you put your intention towards.

Is Entrepreneurship easy? Certainly not. And we do not allude to the fact that following Christ alone enables us to be successful in such an endeavor. What it does secure is our identity, our hope everlasting, and our supernatural guidance directed through signs, solutions, and wonders established by our Father in heaven.

By reading this book and saying yes to being a Joy-full Entrepreneur, you aren't just doing this for you … you aren't just learning for you … you aren't just reading for you…. You are investing in every person you will interact with throughout your life. Your community, your family, your children, your clients … each and every one of them will be better off because of the seeds that will be planted in your soul and the activation thereafter to nurture those seeds.

Remember, even our tombstone won't talk about what we do, it will more profoundly notate who we are. This is a book about becoming who you were always meant to be, by pursuing the One who created you to serve in the unique way only you can do. This is joy-full living.

Reading preparation:

Each chapter features a different Joy-full Entrepreneur who answers multiple questions in order to provide a breath of experience and insight into their responses, rhythms, and research. They will vary with testimonials and are tactically driven to support and equip you.

My favorite way to read this isn't front to back—but actually question by question through each author. There were eleven questions to choose from, and each author chose those that met them best. As you dissect the responses, this methodology will help you have a full understanding of a concept through the lens of multiple teachers. Afterward, I then make space to sit with the Lord to ponder my revelations in reference to His Word and journal how I can strategically apply the wisdom.

Here is the reference to the questions presented (everyone answered #1):

1. Would you describe your entrepreneurial adventure as a **solution, a sign, or a wonder** based on your personal testimony and experience?
   - Testimonies of Transformation
     » Entrepreneurs share whether they perceive their entrepreneurial adventure as a solution, a sign, or a wonder based on their personal testimony and experience.
     » Explore the profound ways in which their entrepreneurial journey has been a catalyst for transformation and divine intervention.

2. What Christ-like **solutions** have you discovered that make your day-to-day business manageable and fruitful?
   - Christ-like Solutions: Managing and Growing a Fruitful Business

» Identify the Christ-like solutions that entrepreneurs have discovered, enabling them to navigate their day-to-day business operations effectively.

» Learn practical strategies for incorporating faith-based principles into the management and growth of a fruitful business.

3. What **signs** have been given to you along the way that have led you to say yes to exploring and activating your entrepreneurial spirit?
   - Signs that Say Yes: Activating the Entrepreneurial Spirit
     » Delve into the signs and signals that entrepreneurs have received along their journey, leading them to embrace and explore their entrepreneurial spirit.
     » Uncover the role of divine guidance and supernatural signs in making crucial decisions and pursuing entrepreneurial opportunities.

4. How do you allow **supernatural signs** to direct your path, process, profit plan, and partnerships in business?
   - Supernatural Guidance: Directing Business Path, Process, Profit Plan, and Partnerships
     » Gain insights into how entrepreneurs allow supernatural signs to shape and direct their business path, processes, profit plans, and partnerships.
     » Learn how faith and divine guidance can influence key decisions and foster alignment with a higher purpose.

5. How is **"wonder"** a part of your rhythm as a leader, visionary, and business builder?
   - Wonder as a Leadership and Visionary Element
     » How wonder is incorporated into the rhythm of being a leader, visionary, and business builder.

> » Exploring the transformative power of embracing wonder and its impact on entrepreneurial success.

6. What does being a **joy-full entrepreneur** mean to you, and how is this emphasized in your daily life?
   - The Joy-Full Entrepreneur: Emphasizing Joy in Daily Life
     > » Defining what it means to be a Joy-full Entrepreneur and how it is emphasized in daily life.
     > » Insights on cultivating joy as an entrepreneur and the positive impact it has on business and personal well-being.

7. Who biblically has been a consistent mentor in your pursuit of excellence as an entrepreneur? What are their unique character traits, and how have they modeled being a **joy-full entrepreneur** well?
   - Biblical Mentors: Models of Joy-Full Entrepreneurship
     > » Highlighting biblical mentors who have consistently inspired and guided entrepreneurs in their pursuit of excellence.
     > » Exploring the unique character traits of these mentors and how they have modeled Joy-Full Entrepreneurship.

8. What has been your biggest challenge or trial in **keeping your joy** as an entrepreneur and leader?
   - Overcoming Challenges: Keeping Joy as an Entrepreneur
     > » Entrepreneurs discuss their biggest challenges or trials in maintaining joy as leaders and entrepreneurs.
     > » Strategies, lessons learned, and wisdom for overcoming obstacles and preserving joy in the face of adversity.

9. How has your **faith** been sharpened as an entrepreneur?
   - Sharpened Faith: Faith's Role in Entrepreneurship

» How faith has been sharpened and deepened through the entrepreneurial journey.

» Testimonies of how faith has sustained and guided entrepreneurs through challenges and successes.

10. How do you **market your business and faith**? What is your belief system in showcasing one over the other, and how have you come to peace with your personal solution?

- Marketing Business and Faith: Finding Personal Solutions
    » Entrepreneurs share their belief systems and strategies for effectively showcasing their business and faith.
    » Insights on finding peace and alignment between personal beliefs and marketing approaches.

11. What wisdom or encouragement would you give someone who has never blended their **faith and business strategy** as one? How has it aided in your profitability?

- Blending Faith and Business: Wisdom for Beginners
    » Practical wisdom and encouragement for those who have yet to blend their faith and business strategies.
    » Exploring the benefits and profitability that arise from integrating faith into entrepreneurial endeavors.

May this book bless you, your business, your entrepreneurial journey, your ministry, your disciples, and the nations in which you are uniquely purposed to serve JOYFULLY!

Publish his glorious deeds among the nations. Tell everyone about the amazing things he has done.

1 Chronicles 16:24, NLT.

Tamra Andress

Tamra Andress is a five-time, best-selling author (five books, two forewords—this is her sixth!), international speaker, top .3% globally seasoned podcaster in spiritual and business categories (*The F.I.T. in Faith Podcast*), and a recognized thought-leader in spiritual entrepreneurship. She is an ordained minister in the marketplace and spends her time speaking, coaching, and hosting events, retreats, and conferences. She is also the founder of F.I.T. in Faith Media, a business and broadcasting company that catalyzes mission-driven leaders through podcasting, publishing (F.I.T. Press), and platform development—ultimately selling words! The founder of The Founder Collective non-profit, established in 2022, serves as a collaboration zone for other faith-driven entrepreneurs to commune and be discipled and equipped through weekly gatherings, experiential retreats, and an annual conference—with sights on an integrated faith and business collision school. Tamra, her husband, and their two children reside in Virginia Beach, VA, but you'll likely see them traveling the globe in their bathing suits!

Chapter 1
Mics, Bikes, and Stages—Oh My!

Would you describe your entrepreneurial adventure as a solution, a sign, or a wonder based on your personal testimony and experience? Explain.

I sat in Nosara, Costa Rica, processing the handful of women from around the United States who were about to land in another country, some for the first time, and I prayed to God, "What do they need?" He deposited two words that cemented into my soul as the fixed non-negotiables of this adventure of entrepreneurship. Hold space with me for a minute—these two words can be light or they can be heavy, depending on your season of life, your circumstance, your lens, or your health.

> *DESIRE and WONDER*
> *"I want you to teach them about desire and wonder,"*
> *He said.*

Well … that was intriguing, and in a place with palms and monkeys and turtles and waterfalls, that felt easy. But I have learned enough about the Lord to know that what appears light-hearted and surface level always has a deep wisdom root. As I explored alongside these women in that inti-

mate retreat setting, I realized that our focused energy on wonder, blended with desire, could put us into a bind and ultimately become strongholds depending on Who or What was guiding our desires and wonder.

Wonder has gotten me into predicaments in my past (explained fully in my first #1 best-selling book, *Always Becoming*), but it's also gotten me out of those same pits. Desires from the flesh have led me to death, and desires from the Spirit have led me to life.

Just as the Word teaches us that our hearts are deceitful in Jeremiah 17:9, it then turns around in Psalm 37:4 (CEV) and says, "Do what the Lord wants, and he will give you your heart's desire." It's only in a renewed heart in Christ that we become aligned to His heart's desire.

The entrepreneurial adventure is the same. You can invest your desire and wonder in your flesh (which I have—pride, ego, greed, and lust, to name a few) and your time stamp here on Earth in moments of satisfaction, or you can invest it in Him, and He will extend your tent pegs, amplify your zeal, and bring you sustenance that far outweighs what the world can give.

Remaining in our child-like faith requires desire, curiosity, and wonder.

> *I praise you, for I am fearfully and wonderfully made.*
> *Wonderful are your works; my soul knows it very well*
> (Psalm 139:14, ESV).

Wonder-FULL like joy-FULL.

> *For to us a child is born, to us a son is given; and the government*
> *shall be upon his shoulder, and his name shall be called Wonderful*
> *Counselor, Mighty God, Everlasting Father, Prince of Peace*
> (Isaiah 9:6, ESV).

He is our wonder-FULL counselor.

We get to be full of wonder each and every day, and I am grateful that my previous intentions, aspirations, and eagerness for worldly outcomes (that have become cultural norms) do not have strongholds on me anymore. And I know you are reading this with the same eagerness and lightness to discover more of what He has in store for you.

What Christ-like solutions have you discovered that make your day-to-day business manageable and fruitful?

The initial element in understanding the solutions that I've discovered requires that we first unpack the shift in mindset and heart set toward what it is that we actually "do" as entrepreneurs each day. The variability between doing and being is a huge piece to it all and requires a lot of inner identity work rather than just external "leadership" development.

Identity work allows us to lay down the titles, the lapel name tags, the email signatures, and bios and pick up our only true and everlasting expression—child. Jehovah Nissi means "The Lord is My Banner." It only occurs once in the Bible as a combination between Jehovah (Yahweh), which is the most used name of God in the Bible, and the Hebrew word *banner* or *flag* (Exodus 17:15). The Israelites used this saying to identify themselves as the unified followers of God. If we were to all walk around with the same banner, the same title, oh, how different organizational charts and board meetings would be.

Now don't get me wrong. I am a massive advocate for leadership; I understand that there are those that go ahead. But even though Moses led Joshua and David led Solomon, ultimately, they each had a banner over them. I've found that the solutions to any area of concern carry an entirely new weight and responsibility of honor in this representation of "being" within the banner. This is true equality and inclusion. This is where we all commune as one. So whether leading a team or a community, stewarding millions or just beginning, part of being a joy-full entrepreneur is the humbling of self to exist as the body.

Once our identity and "being-ness" is in check (and believe me, this is a daily yielding of flesh), the next shift that's most importantly connected to your day-to-day unforced rhythms of grace (Matthew 11:28–30) comes down to perspective and intention.

Are we *managing* our day-to-day, or are we *stewarding* it?

Management often has a hierarchical connectivity, and the associated responsibility involves directing, organizing, and catalyzing movement towards goals and targets while maintaining focus on resources. Conversely, stewardship is the recognition of responsibility with a care towards the relationships, resources, and long-term outcomes of said initiatives. When I shifted from achievement based existing to prioritized holistic synergy in the process, the solutions became clear.

Bountiful fruit must be intentionally stewarded through attention, hydration, exposure, and access. When we lose our scope; overwhelm, grind, hustle, doing, and busyness take precedence, and our eagerness spoils the fruit before it's had time to mature. Ironically, in 2019, I chose *fruitful* as the focus word for my next birth calendar year. It proved to be a comical growth pattern with God. He gave me pomegranates and coconuts … you know, the fruits that are impossible to open, the ones you never really know how to eat or even if they are actually delicious or not because you seem to put all your time and effort into just opening them. So my year did end with fruit, but I didn't get to truly indulge. This was the year that my company sky-rocketed in revenue, engagements, community growth, and global exposure for my podcast. And granted, these were all amazing things, but it was the next year, when the word *maturity* was chosen, that mindsets shifted and solutions were revealed. Interestingly enough, I didn't choose it in connection to fruitfulness at all. The Lord revealed this word in multiple biblical readings, my pastoral message that Sunday, and in conversation with my hubby who is also a business mentor in many ways. So maturation set in, and I realized it was in that place, those next steps and seasons of nurturing said growth, that I unlocked stewardship rather than management and the character traits needed to be an effective leader and entrepreneur.

So in a nut-shell (maybe a coconut-shell because it wasn't a quick and easy discovery), if I were to encourage you through Christ-like solutions you should rest in for effective "management," they would be:

- Choose Identity over Titles (recommendation: *The End of Me* by Kyle Idleman).
- Apply Rhythms of Grace over Grind (recommendation: *Grace Over Grind* by Shae Bynes).
- Learn to steward vs. manage through pace, care, attention to detail, and holistic effort (especially when dealing with people).
- Choose an intention or word over your year (recommendation: *One Word That Will Change Your Life* by Dan Britton, Jon Gordon, and Jimmy Page).

All of which derive from time in the Word and relationship with Christ!

> *Religion teaches you to manage;*
> *Christ teaches us to steward.*

What signs have been given to you along the way that have led you to say yes to exploring and activating your entrepreneurial spirit?

I was handed a microphone in front of cameras and lights for the first time when I was seven. I was in front of hundreds in school assemblies giving speeches by the time I was ten. I served on the board of the mayor's youth council by the time I was twelve. I was the only freshman in the city hand-picked to attend the executive board of their high school student government while still in middle school. I helped start a nonprofit before I was twenty-one. I may not have started official kid-preneur initiatives, but our mission-driven work in cultivating movements, raising money, hosting events, leading marketing campaigns, and gathering community has been ingrained and activated since I was young.

After business school at James Madison University, I started the entrepreneurial endeavors that led to nearly two decades and eleven business initiatives later, which puts us here today. Were there signs to lead me? There were always doors opening. There was belief and empowerment from adults who hardly knew me. There were extended hands from principals and administrators that pushed me higher. There were coaches who didn't let me sit complacent in a skill or role. So yes, sure. But there were also naysayers, bullies, closed doors, missed opportunities, selfish desires, and comparison traps that left me void in the climb.

Without Jesus, I wouldn't be here. I wouldn't even be alive. His spirit guides and provides signs—the intuitive pull between right and left, the gut check of decisions and partnerships, the God-winks from strangers and nature, the dreams and visions that come to fruition.

Without signs I'd be stagnant. Without correlated "coincidences," as most may call them, I'd be lost. Without other guiding lights that keep me confidently moving towards the direction of my eternity, I'd be isolated. Without Truth tellers speaking out loud in the marketplace, I'd call myself crazy. But, hey, John the Baptist and Paul were called crazy … but a little crazy only lights a fire or two! I want to light millions of soul-fires. So I'm eyes, ears, and heart open to all the signs.

What does being a joy-full entrepreneur mean to you and how is this emphasized in your daily life?

Just as with the banner I mentioned earlier, there are many other coined phrases used by Christ followers who are also entrepreneurs. We hyphenate things like faith-based entrepreneur or kingdom-entrepreneur or Christian-business owner, which I totally utilize and market as well, but to what end?

If our actions are not meeting our marketing, then we are showcasing a broken system. The hustle-hard, sleep under your desk, forget your meals, and mis-prioritization of family do not portray that you are pursu-ing Jesus, even though it's posted and featured as if it's pursuing purpose. Purpose and Jesus are not the same thing. I'm committed to my purpose because I love Jesus. I can break commitments to Jesus, but Jesus will never break covenant with God. So when I position my joy and my overflowing fullness of love from Christ as the banner and covenant of my day-to-day, my commitments follow that Truth versus the other way around.

Matthew 12:34 (ESV) says, "For out of the abundance of the heart the mouth speaks." This is why I start my day pursuing the Joy-Full One who makes my joy cup full. My time with the Lord in the morning, cozied up in my fireplace corner with my warm mug, allows me to bring my worries, my day, my questions, my hopes, and my needed decisions to the One who has predestined my good works for me. (Such a different flow from those who are entrepreneurs that just happen to be Christian.) And everything from our team meetings, to my podcast shows (*The F.I.T. in Faith Podcast*), speaking engagements, new author conversations, retreats, and conferences are sealed in prayer whether at opening or closing. This allows the joy to flow from me to others. Where is your allegiance? Is your commitment to your career superseding your covenant relationship with Christ? (I have to ask myself this question often, so no condemnation.)

And while we don't always get it perfect, we serve The Perfect One who loves us even still. To paraphrase a popular jingle by the band Cain that plays in our car and home regularly—even on my worst days and even on my best days, I'm a child of God. And ultimately, no day is a bad day because He's the reason why we're so blessed!

> *Being a joy-full entrepreneur is not a selfish endeavor to earn, it's a selfless opportunity to serve.*

What has been your biggest challenge or trial in keeping your joy as an entrepreneur and leader?

I have two mirrored scenarios that have left a bit of a scar. And while I don't hold offense (thanks to John Bevere's book *The Bait of Satan* and Lysa Terkeurst's *Forgiving What You Can't Forget*), they still carry weight for me because of my own heart brokenness and the brokenness of those that were hurt and taken advantage of in a similar way (most still without full recognition).

You see, as the leader of an organization, you can also become entrusted as the spiritual leader as well (which isn't necessarily a good or bad thing but must be taken note of). When this occurs, team members, community leaders, clients, and even friends won't speak up the same as they may have in the past, especially if you aren't asking their opinion.

Side note: God's voice matters most, but He's likely also gifted you trusted confidants at your side to help you maneuver through. We cannot become self-reliant, and spiritual mentorship, especially in the category of discernment, is a critical aid.

The two challenges came years apart but, in hindsight, wearing similar wolf-like clothing. We are shepherds, after all, and if our flock gets hurt, we are held responsible. My eagerness and my excitability can get the best of me when opportunities arise, especially when presented as "God-orchestrated" scenarios. Spiritual manipulation is running rampant in society from churches to businesses alike, and people can use the Word of God to their advantage to extend their reach, to pressure to buy, to twist arms into giving, and ultimately to build their empire—not the kingdom of God. I wear my heart on my sleeve, and I trust easily, which might sound self-righteous, but I mean it humbly and sometimes with frustration as well.

I have had to learn that while I pray heavily into discernment and guidance, I need to also yield to advisers. It wasn't until the rug was pulled out from under me and many others were bruised by third-party interactions that I could even see the forest for the trees. I now have people who are chosen mentors, people that I can go to for a different perspective, a gut check, and insight into what God is telling them before I make big leaps of "faith" that end up being big leaps into messes. When that happens, I know that God will pick me up and dust me back off, but not everyone is so easily ignited back to their joy. And that's where patience, communication, renewed trust, and prayer will be our biggest assets to mending what can be broken.

The maturity I mentioned earlier did come into play, however, before the second situation unfolded. I spent seven days on a water-only fast waiting to hear from God. It wasn't until two days after that fast that He gave me, in abundance, what I was hoping for—signs of why I should make the next move, even if it was uncomfortable and risked relationships and money and wasted months of time and energy. In the end, it was worth it, and much was salvaged through that decision.

These friction points have been connected to "partnership"—and while I am completely an advocate of the body operating as one, there are a few things to make note of as a front line of defense moving forward:

1. Look to their fruit. "Beware of false prophets, who come to you in sheep's clothing, but inwardly they are ravenous wolves. You will know them by their fruits. Do men gather grapes from thornbushes or figs from thistles? Even so, every good tree bears good fruit, but a bad tree bears bad fruit. A good tree cannot bear bad fruit, nor can a bad tree bear good fruit. Every tree that does not bear good fruit is cut down and thrown into the fire. Therefore by their fruits you will know them" (Matthew 7:15–20, NKJV).

2. Ask more questions—of God, of your confidants, of your team, of the potential partner, of their previous colleagues and relationships.

3. Trust who they show you they are. There will be red flags, warning signs, misguided scenarios, gut checks—do not ignore them when they occur.

And ultimately, we have to follow the third principle in the list above that most forget.

Those we partner with can't just be like-minded or like-hearted, they have to be like-handed. God's children do not have a scarcity mentality and are not greedy. And if you get burned … just remember we serve a God of justice, and He preserves the faithful. What you may have seemingly lost will return to you multiplied. Keep your joy-light on.

Challenges met with signs and finished with wonders and solutions have led to the growth of this company. There will be more … and I will say "Yes" to God, not man.

How has your faith been sharpened as an entrepreneur?

A lot of apparel and swag these days display the phrase *faith over fear*, but faith in spite of fear is more often the equation. Fortunately, it only has to be the size of a mustard seed to warrant a response from God that can move a mountain. The disciples were proof of this time and time again. I love how *The Chosen* television series personifies the Gospels as well as the disciples in their response to being gifted the Spirit and sent out two by two to perform miracles (Mark 6:7–13). Their faces were simultaneously struck with shock and joy. They weren't sure they could heal the sick or the lame or cast out demons, but they simply had faith that He could because He had shown them no other Truth but that He was who He said He was.

Honestly, I don't know how these big visions are going to come to fruition. I often don't even know who the next contract will be from or if the next planned experience will be over-budget or abundant. And though we can project and plan all day long, most days, in all transparency, I'm just walking in faith—which requires me to release control, stop preparing for what He's prepared me for (gifted reminder from my brother and Pastor Anthony Hart), and learn to more quickly yield to the Holy Spirit.

Questions I've had to face:

- Do I really trust Him?

- Is He really my Provider like He says He is?
- If I fast social media, will I lose my business?
- Did I make this up? Is it my will or your will, Lord?
- What if I fail? Will God be disappointed?
- Is this supposed to get bigger? Do I hire other people?
- Do you really not want me to take a penny? (My next book is on this!)
- Am I worthy?
- Who am I to be entrusted with this?

Here are the ways my faith has been sharpened:

1. Gaining biblical knowledge through reading, writing, and teaching
2. Staying steadfast in the face of family and friends who don't see the vision
3. Seeing God work in mighty ways through blessings
4. Trusting His timing and pace

How do you market your business and faith? What is your belief system in showcasing one over the other and how have you come to peace with your personal solution?

In 2022, after my morning devotional time, I walked into my garage gym, and the Lord told me to "speak now." I pondered this statement because as a speaker, podcaster, and coach, I literally talk all the time. He said, "No, now. Teach right now." I was at a loss and selfishly and childishly went back and forth with God. "This is my time to train and listen to my books or podcasts. It's my time to learn." But as I'm sure you've experienced before, He didn't let up. So I propped up my phone and climbed up on my stationary bike. I had nothing planned, no idea what I was going to talk about. In my head I said, "Ok, fifteen minutes." Isn't it comical how we set time limits and issue ultimatums to God?

An hour later I stopped the ride. I had laughed, cried, received Holy-Spirit downloads, said things I'd never said out loud before, and taught things I'd never taught before. I watched the live viewers comment, and honestly, while it was only a few that participated … it didn't matter. I had never felt so free to SPEAK.

I didn't have to plan. I didn't have to prepare. I didn't need an outline or notes because God was working through me. In volume 1 of *The Joy-full Entrepreneur*, I share my first experience on stage where the Lord silenced me before my keynote address and the freedom that came on the other side of obedience. Ultimately, that's the question being asked here because, if you read scripture, there is no separation of marketplace and ministry. It is one and the same. And God is calling us up and out. He's telling His children to testify. He's sending us. After all, it's the Great Commission. And there's never been a more ripe time for harvest!

If we hold our knowledge of freedom for ourselves, especially in our workplace, where we exist one-third of our waking hours, aren't we then existing as the lukewarm church that Paul warned us against? This is the reason we launched our nonprofit, The Founder Collective. Through this endeavor, joy-full entrepreneurs could freely come together to support one another—no longer as strangers but as co-heirs with Christ—as His children, on a firm foundation with Him as our CEO so we would not stand alone but truly be the church mobilized as one in Him.

So then you are no longer strangers and aliens, but you are fellow citizens with the saints and members of the household of God, built on the foundation of the apostles and prophets, Christ Jesus himself being the cornerstone, in whom the whole structure, being joined together, grows into a holy temple in the Lord. In him you also are being built together into a dwelling place for God by the Spirit (Eph. 2:19–22, ESV).

You may not jump on a bike and go live and preach multiple times a week (but you should totally join me!); you may not pray with your whole staff (though I highly recommend it); you may not have a cross hanging in your office (not needed) ... but scripture says it best in Matthew 10:33 (NLT): "But everyone who denies me here on earth, I will also deny before my Father in heaven." I totally understand that not every industry, role, or regulation set before us allows us to be so vibrant in our constitutional freedom of speech, so there is no judgment in choice here, but I do believe you know when and where and how you can enhance your vocalization practices and "speak now!" too.

Nothing about the call of marketplace ministry is easy, and it is not exclusive to an entrepreneur. It is our role as leaders in our community to train up our managers, teams, and even communities and clients to recognize their role in operating as the mobilized church. Jesus is still our perfect example of how to walk into uncommon places to love, teach, and be the light that provides peace through training while applying tangibility with solutions, signs, and wonders and never forgetting the power of prayer. As we embark on the daily adventure of Joy-full Entrepreneurship, our hearts must be postured in humility, patient to yield, and expectant for divine signs, solutions, and wonders too. He goes before us.

*The Founder Collective meets for weekly discipleship meetings, open forum, to discuss scriptural leadership, marriage, entrepreneurship, and truly anything the Spirit guides us to discuss. I encourage you, regardless of your public display of Christ, to find a trusted group that can partner with you in your pursuit. We are all in pursuit of operating as Joy-full Entrepreneurs. thefoundercollective.org/foundertable

*You're invited to take a seat at the table.

But that's not all! Even in times of trouble we have a joyful confidence, knowing that our pressures will develop in us patient endurance. And patient endurance will refine our character, and proven character leads us back to hope. And this hope is not a disappointing fantasy, because we can now experience the endless love of God cascading into our hearts through the Holy Spirit who lives in us!

Romans 5:3–5, TPT.

Angela Bellar

Angela Bellar is a leading industry marketer in health and wellness, a John Maxwell certified coach, motivational speaker, and top podcaster. With eighteen years of experience as a registered nurse, she's an overcomer of interpersonal violence, chronic illness, and trauma. Angela is a true entrepreneur, building multiple six-figure businesses and coaching a team of 3000 for three years.

Her strength lies in her unwavering faith and reliance on God's guidance. Having triumphed over her own struggles, she's committed her life to inspiring and empowering women to find their true identity through the promises of God. From the stage to hosting women's retreats, her magnetic presence inspires others to understand their worth at every stage of life.

Angela's expertise isn't limited to marketing and coaching; she's a podcasting sensation, reaching millions with her wisdom and laughter. She's a personal brand strategist, transforming closets into brands, showcasing her limitless creativity.

Leading by example, Angela lives by the motto: More Serving, Less Selling. Her genuine care for others sets her apart as a mentor and friend. With unwavering passion and dedication, she guides women to embrace their potential, offering the actual steps needed to find rescue, redemption, and restoration in the presence of God.

In Angela Bellar, you'll find an unstoppable force of inspiration, propelling you to a life filled with purpose, joy, and unshakeable faith. Get ready to soar with Angela as your guide!

Chapter 2
Going Through

Would you describe your entrepreneurial adventure as a solution, a sign, or a wonder based on your personal testimony and experience? Explain.

I would explain my entrepreneurial adventure as just that, a true adventure and a WONDER. I stumbled into it at a time when I thought my story was over. You see, I wondered how I would ever get better, IF I would ever get better. After my third child, I was struck with Lupus. In the end, I was on fourteen medications, malnourished, depressed, and desperate. I was carrying a wheelchair in my car and fighting for my life on a daily basis. Oddly enough, it wasn't that I believed in healing for myself, the answers came through my belief in healing for my youngest daughter. She had been diagnosed with migraines and an autoimmune condition at just two years old. Witnessing her suffering prompted me to cry out to God, asking Him to give her pain to me. I began to lean into the healing power of God in a whole new way because I knew that was the only solution for my daughter. One morning I said, "Abi, guess what? God can heal you. Do you believe that?" She responded that she did. And in that moment, she and I committed to praying and believing daily for that healing.

It was a Wednesday night at a little country church east of Nashville, and Abi was standing just to my left. There was one cowboy on stage with a guitar, and he was singing "Victory In Jesus." Expecting nothing, we worshiped. During the second chorus while I sang, "I heard about His healing," the power of God washed over me. I felt like I had just swallowed warm honey as the sensation flowed down my neck and chest. I reached my left hand over and put it on Abi's sweet head. At that moment, the Holy Spirit said, "It's done."

"What, wait, what just happened?" I thought to myself. I told no one! That night at bedtime, she had no symptoms, the next day, none, the next and the next, NONE. After three days, I said to her dad, "Have you noticed that Abi hasn't had symptoms in three days?" He responded, "Now that you mention it, yes!" I told him what happened, and the Spirit confirmed the healing to him as well. That was six years ago, and she has not suffered a symptom since. Can I get an AMEN!?

After encountering her healing, I started asking the Lord if He would heal me too! Think about what *wonder* means. It's a feeling of surprise mingled with admiration, caused by something unexpected, unfamiliar, inexplicable, and beautiful. And to my great wonder, in that same church, only months later, a woman introduced me to what would become the springboard for not just healing my body but the pathway to healing my soul! I often say, "When you think you are going to die and you don't, you live differently."

What Christ-like solutions have you discovered that make your day-to-day business manageable and fruitful?

Christ-like solutions have certainly been the basis of what makes my business manageable and fruitful day-to-day. Shortly after "accidentally" starting a business, I realized that personal growth and leadership skills would definitely be required if I wanted to succeed and scale my business. What I find so interesting, even just typing this, is the preparation that God afforded me before the opportunity actually came. He was preparing me throughout all the years I spent in obscurity. One of my favorite quotes is from renowned motivational speaker, Les Brown: "It's better to be prepared for an opportunity and not have one, than to have an opportunity and not be prepared."

I can sincerely say that every solution for the management and fruitfulness of my business has come from Christ. He has been the ultimate leader and example, and I could write an entire book on the number of solutions He provided for me in just the last five years of my business. I have a firm belief that there is not a question in the world that we won't find the answer to in God's Word. And while I have not gone to seminary and do not have a theological degree, I have been a student of the Word of God, and it has been my source for more than twenty-five years. I have seen Him honor His Word, rescue His people, redeem them, and prepare them. I know I can trust His leading. Proverbs 16:3 (ESV) says, "Commit your work to the LORD, and your plans will be established."

The most important decision I made in my business was having Him be the CEO. I have journals full of our meetings. Spending that time with Him allowed me to function on the next right step principle. When overwhelm would come in like a flood, I would say to myself, "The Lord has gone before me to make preparation for everything I need before I get there." Sometimes I said that once a day and other times one hundred times a day. He doesn't give us ALL the steps that it will take, but He does provide the next right step, and He is faithful. I committed with firm resolve to BELIEVE that, in putting Him first, He would give me the direction I needed.

One of the many revelations God has given me that you can put into action at any time is simple systems. I was asking Him to help me lead in a way that was simple and replicable when He spoke, "Simple Systems." After hearing that, I began to look closer at the systems in my business. I looked at them one by one and broke each of them down into a strategy with no more than three steps. God does not over complicate things, like I can tend to do. Simple systems in your business will bring clarity and help you preserve your bandwidth for creating more and more. This is a process, so take that first step. Evaluate your systems; break them down into three parts or steps; fill in the gaps, if there are systems you need to create; and then feel the peace and ease that comes from this organization.

What signs have been given to you along the way that have led you to say yes to exploring and activating your entrepreneurial spirit?

I LOVE that we can trust the Lord to reveal where He wants us to be and when He wants us to be there. Initially, I would not have said, "I am called to speak." But I knew in my heart that I was. I had never told another person because fear was holding me captive. If I said I wanted to speak, then I would have to stand up and do that. The thought of it terrified me, but the vision never left me. Have you been there—in that place of knowing God has called you to do something and at the same time not being able to see the possibility of that thing?

So I sat with the Lord and said, "If you want me to speak, I will." We had a deal, lol. I promised God that, if I were asked to speak, my answer would be yes! Within the next month, several opportunities presented themselves, and I said, "yes." I got on those stages scared, brand new, and OPEN to the calling.

I believe God leads and directs us through His Word and will at times provide a sign in order to build our faith in the direction He is calling us. For me, many of these "signs" have come through divine appointments. The divine connections He has provided me are far too many to share here. In order to step into those places, I have had to choose to live with an open heart. Living with an open heart sounds nice, but, if you've ever been hurt, you know it is no simple task. Living with an open heart means trusting His leading. A few years ago, the next right step for me was trusting the Lord as He said, "Get in the room." I went to more than fifteen events, retreats, and conferences that year during the Covid shutdown. Why would God ask me to do the opposite of what the world was doing? For me, that was a sign.

While getting in the room, the Lord revealed so many things that were necessary for me to learn in order to activate and take my business to all new levels. I believe God orchestrated that season to direct me to see clearly which rooms He wanted me in AND the ones that were not for me. I walked into rooms where I knew no one, and that pressed me to walk with confidence in a whole new way. I walked into rooms full of leaders and successful entrepreneurs, and that caused me to level up in my own business. I walked into rooms surrounded by people I knew and loved in order to inspire them to grow and take courageous steps in their own businesses. It was a time of stretching and growing personally in order to navigate the incredible things that were to come.

What signs have you seen for your business? I encourage you to be open to seeing the signs God is using in your life to direct you and prepare you for the next level. We can trust the spiritual signs in our lives and watch our faith activate and grow!

What does being a joy-full entrepreneur mean to you and how is this emphasized in your daily life?

Being a joy-full entrepreneur means going for LIFE! I asked myself several years ago, "What brings me life, and what brings me death?" I decided to go for life! American singer, songwriter, and actor, Marc Anthony said, "If you do what you love, you'll never work a day in your life." That sounds great, but how do you actually see that in your life? How do you make that happen? I believe it is by evaluating what you do daily and asking yourself what brings you life. Once you know the answer to that question, you can begin to make the decisions necessary to orchestrate your business for more of what you want and less of what you don't want. I have a deep belief in living WHOLE, so in my list I included body, mind, and spirit. Here is an example of how I started making this list:

- Passion and Purpose (Spirit): Engaging in activities that align with your passions, interests, and values is crucial. I woke up daily with a calling on my heart and mind and needed to lean into that calling to search out where God was leading me.

- Relationships (Mind): Having meaningful connections with family, friends, and loved ones bring joy, support, and a sense of belonging. The power of connection and community cannot be overlooked or undervalued.
- Growth and Learning (Mind): Prioritizing personal growth and development has become a part of my everyday life. I knew I had to unlearn being chronically ill, and as John Maxwell says, "Personal growth takes long looks in the mirror." My personal growth is my personal decision each day. We grow in our relationship with God and in our personal lives through the renewing of our minds.
- Health and Wellness (Body): Suffering from illness and being unable to work resulted in me selling my business. I had heard, "Your health is your wealth," and I have found that to be true. Taking care of my health and leading others to do the same are fundamental to my ability to create success. I do not take my health for granted and have created daily habits to make my ongoing health a priority.
- Creativity and Expression (Spirit): Learning to access, express, and give away my creativity has been life changing. For many years I said I wasn't creative, but I have learned that my creativity is different from what I was taught and thought was creative. I love to decorate, and that is creativity. It is creativity to design Airbnbs. I love fashion and using creativity to design other brands and mine! My mother always said that I could walk in a room, turn around three times, and everything would be beautiful.

Some things that can lead to death:

- Negative Relationships: Living with toxic or unhealthy relationships will drain your energy, cause stress, or hinder personal growth. This can have a detrimental effect on YOU being the "Youiest YOU." I had to allow God to sift and sort relationships in my life to help me see the truth about the health of those relationships.

- Unfulfilling Work: Working a job or career that you find uninteresting, unsatisfying, or devoid of purpose can negatively impact your overall sense of fulfillment and joy. You CAN do what you love! If work feels draining, ask the Lord to lead you to your passion and purpose.

- Neglecting Physical and Mental Health: Ignoring your physical and mental well-being, engaging in unhealthy habits, or neglecting self-care can have a negative impact on your quality of life. My first business coach started with self-care … I remember thinking, "What? How could that be the most important thing to work on?" I have since found that this IS the most important place to start.

- Fear and Limiting Beliefs: Allowing fear, self-doubt, or limiting beliefs to control your actions can prevent personal growth and restrict you from pursuing what truly brings you life. On my journey of personal growth and development, I found that "playing small," was a huge issue in my life. I wanted everyone around me to be COMFORTABLE, so I dimmed my light to help them feel better or to keep them from competing with me.

Understanding what brings me life and what brings me death has been vital in my entrepreneurial adventure. John 10:10 (TPT) says, "A thief has only one thing in mind—he wants to steal, slaughter, and destroy. But I have come to give you everything in abundance, more than you expect—Life in its fullest until you overflow!"

What has been your biggest challenge or trial in keeping your joy as an entrepreneur and leader?

I like to talk about challenges. Keeping my joy as an entrepreneur has not been an easy task. They say, "It's simple, but not easy." I feel that so deeply in my journey. I heard bestselling author, coach, and speaker, John

Maxwell, say over and over, "Fail forward, fail fast, and fail often." My first business coach asked me a question that I now ask my clients: "Are you willing to take imperfect action to have your dreams?" I paused for a moment and thought, "Yeah, let's go!" I learned through the trials in my life that life didn't have to be perfect to be wonderful, and that was such a release for me. I was released to dream, to fail, to learn, and to grow. Perfection was not the requirement. But unfortunately, it was instilled in me at a very young age. I was the second oldest and the only girl, and being "perfect" was what had always gotten me the recognition that I needed. So how do I unlearn this habit? How do I do it messy and expect others to follow that example?

"It's not about you!" I was sitting with my grandfather one day when he taught me a life lesson that I wouldn't use for years to come. He said, "What do your friends think about you?" I started naming all the things they thought. I responded, "She thinks I am smart." "She doesn't like me." "He doesn't think I am pretty ..." My grandfather leaned back in his chair and listened, and then he was quiet. He finally responded, "They aren't thinking about you ..." I was appalled! Of course they were thinking about me, and I knew what they were thinking. As I looked back on this conversation, I realized what he was trying to teach me. Other people are too busy thinking about themselves to think about me. In other words, do what you are going to do, and don't worry about what others think because it's probably NOT about you.

This gave me freedom to venture into what God called me to do without thinking about what others thought, approved of, or validated. I continue to see (for me and so many others) that comparison, playing small, and limiting ourselves to what others approve of is what holds us back from chasing our dreams, living in our fullest potential, and choosing the creativity God has placed in our hearts. I have heard that "Comparison is the thief of joy," but I say, "Comparison is the thief of identity." I believe fully that I have something to display on this planet that no one else can display. I believe YOU have a purpose on this planet, and I don't want to see that hindered by what others approve of or validate. Finding JOY in the journey is being exactly who you were created to be and doing exactly what you were called to do.

Closing Thoughts

I want to leave you with something the Lord showed me years ago, something that has become the core training of my coaching program and retreats. As my story began to be shared more and more, people asked me how I overcame so much. At first I didn't have awareness of how it was possible, and I asked the Lord that same question. "Lord, how did I overcome so much? Will you reveal it to me so I can give the roadmap to others?" His response was, "You kept growing for it." That is where Grow-4-It was birthed.

The "G" stands for God because everything begins with Him. The "R" is for *resilience*. Most of us don't know how resilient we are until we are faced with things we must endure. The "O" is for *opportunity* and the preparation that is vital before the opportunity arrives as well as the vision to see the opportunities as they appear. The "W" is for *worth*. It is the understanding that you are worthy now, not just when you achieve and the power of understanding your worth in God's sight. The "4" is for the four seasons. It is a reminder that God moves in seasons, and we are always flowing into and out of different seasons in life and in our business. Knowing this brings peace when times are difficult. The "I" is for *identity*. The world is constantly attempting to change our identity. I am _____ is a powerful little statement and will directly impact your divine joy. The "T" is for *trust*. You can trust Him. And learning to trust yourself and the commitments you make on your journey will propel you to places you have only dreamed.

So let's Grow-4-It together and inspire others to do the same.

Many blessings, xoxo, Angela

Commit your works to the Lord
[submit and trust them to Him],
And your plans will succeed
[if you respond to His will
and guidance]

Proverbs 16:3, AMP.

Keith Callaway

Keith L. Callaway is an unabashed follower of Christ, husband of over forty years, father of seven, and grandfather of sixteen (and counting) whose life purpose is to "get wisdom and give wisdom!" He founded a construction business over forty years ago, and, in addition to overseeing the culture of fifty people, he is using the experience to coach other business owners on how to leave a lasting legacy while he mentors his own teams using the motto TRANSFORMING LIVES ONE SHOVEL AT A TIME. He is a best-selling author and uploads a daily devotional to Instagram and YouTube titled *Get to Work Devotional.* In addition, Keith hosts a podcast called *Greatness from Small Beginnings,* where he interviews those that have broken generational cycles or have grown increasingly into their greatest potential.

Fun fact: He has six sons and one daughter. But in an odd twist, God gave him fifteen granddaughters and one grandson (so far)!

Chapter 3
Get to Your Highest and Greatest

Would you describe your entrepreneurial journey as a solution, a sign, or a wonder based on your personal testimony and experience?

Forty years ago when I started in business, I would have had to look in a dictionary to find the meaning of the word *entrepreneur*. As I wrote this, I looked it up, and sure enough, that's me. (I'll let you look it up for yourself to see if it's you as well.) My entrepreneurial path has been a quest peppered with literal life and death experiences and many days of the mundane. It has also been full of so many hilarious happenings that I regret not having kept a journal. It certainly would have made a great sitcom or reality show that many could relate to.

In the beginning, going into business was my reaction to being undervalued at the retail job I held, when I got married. I knew I could do better because I had done door-to-door sales in my early teens, and finding customers didn't seem like a problem to me. So two months after I got married, I set out on my own, and four months after that, I found out I was going to be a dad! At that moment, this adventure to find value took on a new importance. It became my SOLUTION for providing for my growing family.

After seventeen years of grinding through the seasons of business as well as the calendar seasons of each of those seventeen years (outdoor construction was and is extremely weather sensitive), I received a SIGN from

31

God—He wanted it to be more than a SOLUTION…. In September of 2000, I went on a monthlong mission trip to Italy that was very intense in all ways—but especially spiritually. When I returned to my home and my business (that I had left in the hands of the good men who worked for me), I realized what that trip had cost me. Although they did a good job while I was away, the business had suffered. But what suffered most was my sense of purpose! I never in my life had felt such a deep dissatisfaction with the work that I did. Suddenly, paving driveways seemed so worldly and temporal and so far from giving me the fulfillment that mission work brought me—but I had a family to support, right?

About two months after returning from Italy, I set up an appointment with my pastor. The subject matter, I thought, would be the status of the adult Sunday school ministry that I helped to lead. Instead, it was the conversation that changed my outlook completely as to what business means in light of the kingdom. My pastor, Dwight, always asked a particular question to start every meeting, but that day he didn't. He simply asked, "How are you?" Not being one to sugarcoat the truth, I told him of my dissatisfaction that had become frustration and what I felt was a need for change and perhaps a calling to ministry. What he did and said next surprised me and activated the mindset change I needed to see business as ministry.

He was a tall man and during meetings had always sat behind his desk and leaned back in his high-back office chair. But that day, after I answered his question, he leaned forward (what seemed like halfway across the desk) with his elbows planted and both of his long forefingers pointed at my heart and started speaking. "Yes indeed, you are called to ministry in much the same way I am," he said. But you don't want this kind of ministry! You have the privilege AND the ability AND the position to speak to an entire portion of this world that would never set foot in this building and would never listen to me if they did. The men that work for you, your customers, and your suppliers will never receive the message of the gospel from me or anyone like me. But they will receive it from you! I envy your position. You are called! Don't treat that lightly!" I don't remember what else we talked about that day, as you can imagine!

Since that day—my own personal "renewing of your mind" moment (Rom. 12:2 [NIV])—I've increasingly seen my business as a mechanism for transformation and am now teaching that SIGN as a calling to other Christian business owners, starting with my family who are all entrepreneurs.

What Christ-like solutions have you discovered that make your day-to-day business manageable and fruitful?

I have always cared deeply for the people who work with me and for me. I don't think anyone who worked with me would say differently, but I realized after decades of people moving on to greener pastures that just caring about them and not connecting their work to their future made the caring less effective and their work less enjoyable. Five years ago, I realized that since we were already scaling quickly, I needed to take the opportunity to fix that problem. I soon discovered that those who are inspired to grow into their best future within an organization don't leave. Most will actively look for a way to grow into their best self where they are, if possible! "I want all these good people to stay with me for the long haul! I need to give them reasons to stay," I thought.

I did three things to advance this thought. I visualized where we were going as a company, identified who we needed to get there, and prayed for them. Some we already had on board at that point, but many would have to be added. I knew that we needed the right people, but we also needed to be the right fit for their future greatness. I started seeing the futures of my people possibly more clearly than even they did and started communicating what I saw in them, along with encouraging them to talk about what they pictured in their future.

A year or so later (in a conversation completely unrelated to business growth and the bottom line), my oldest son and partner, Keith Jr., and I came up with the idea to take all of our crew guys and salesmen away to a trade conference and equipment expo. "It'll be fun," we said. So we did it! We bought matching shirts for everyone (seventeen people, including Keith Jr. and me) and flew out to Nashville for four days in January, which is our slow season anyway. The results in the months following that trip were astounding. We had almost no bad attitudes, and if we did, their coworkers usually took care of them. The team started cross training, teaching, and trading spots with each other to pick up the slack for anyone who was struggling, and being on time or early to work became the norm. We laughed more often as an entire team and were not intimidated when others were enjoying themselves. We had a cohesion that we had never had before, and the owners/bosses (though clearly in charge) were part of the team and enjoyed their work much more. This connectedness lasted for almost six months, in spite of adding a couple of people to the team, but the long days and heat of the summer took its toll on the "good culture," as I called it.

That lesson was an important one. I realized that a good culture needs constant attention, constant upgrading, constant resets, and constant core values reminders. It needs the constant breeze of inspiration flowing through it. So my next task was to create a cycle of connection points that would continue that good culture, but those connection points would need to focus on two critical components.

The first component required that we recognize that all people want to be "seen"—Jesus saw people. We have incorporated this component in a number of ways. Each week in our team meeting, we encourage everyone to join in a conversation that is prompted by asking a question as an icebreaker. And every couple of weeks we identify a problem that we discuss and solve during the meeting with practical outcomes. We also have our team members set one to three quarterly work goals based on anonymous peer reviews (through the lens of the company core values).

In addition, each year we sit down with each person to set a personal goal using the SMARTER goal setting method. This often initiates a conversation about where they want to be in five to ten years. That personal goal comes with a midyear check-in that asks about the status of their goal. During these check-ins, I hope to hear that they are either on track or that they have revised their goal, and if there is an issue, I ask if there is any way we can help them meet their goal.

We also hold what we call Task Force meetings at least twice a year or when we are having a disconnect between departments. There is representation from all segments of our company at these meetings, and there is an open discussion about how well we are doing or not doing certain tasks. It's not a problem solving time, however, just a transparent conversation. The results from this meeting go to the company's leadership team to help them identify and prevent blind spots.

Another way we ensure that we are "seeing" our people is to stop production for at least a half day once per quarter to have some fun, eat together, and have a company meeting. During this meeting, we read stats, listen to a motivational speech, give cash awards based on core values, and revisit the quarterly and company goals to make sure we are all on the same page regarding the immediate and long term vision. Oh, and by the way, getting on the airplane and going somewhere as a company to do some educational training and/or team building has become part of who we are, and now it includes everybody, both men and women. Many of our team members look forward to this more than any other event. In 2023, it included thirty-nine people!

The second component required that we recognize that all people want to be inspired to grow—Jesus inspired people. And like the kingdom of God, the growth plan of the company would have to be big enough to encompass ALL the personal growth goals of ALL people in the organization as well as what they pictured as their highest and greatest. We made our company growth plan public, and we invite discussion about it and where they fit in, today and in the future.

We believe that (just like feeding hungry people) seeing people's potential and feeding them with opportunities for growth is the biggest first step for them to embrace the truths of the kingdom. If they are starving for growth, they won't see what's really important, which is, of course, a relationship with the author of their purposes on this earth. We as business people need to feed hungry souls, or they will likely not hear the message of the gospel.

How is "wonder" a part of your rhythm as a leader, visionary, and business builder?

Wonder (the word *delight* also comes to mind) has not always been part of my rhythm as a business owner. For almost two decades, I focused solely on providing for my family and not taking risks. But God had made me to be a visionary; I was to build and to lead others to be their highest as I stepped out to find mine. Unfortunately, for years I avoided new opportunities and anything that wasn't under the banner of "Provide, Protect, and Love my family more than everything." Unfortunately, my intentions to do what was "right" ended up creating a poverty mindset that constrained God's delight in me. He wanted to delight in seeing me become my highest and greatest as soon as possible and for as long as possible. And I stopped Him. Was it sin? Mostly no. (The lack of faith may have been.) Was it short sighted? Yes! Do I have a few regrets? Yes!

About seven years into my business, I met a business owner in my line of work (paving and road building) with a business that was much more mature than mine. He offered to mentor me "for a couple of years" and then, perhaps, pass the business along to me. As flattered as I was, I couldn't see this as a good opportunity to consider at the time. A number of concerns filled my head:

- I would have to move two hours away.
- I would have to change churches.
- My kids would have to change schools.
- How much would I make?
- What would my wife think? (So I never asked her.)
- I'm kinda scared, etc.

Do you see anything in that list that was too big or too hard to overcome? No, neither do I ... NOW! But back then my thinking was just too small, and my lack of vision stunted my growth as a person in every possible way. That opportunity may or may not have been for me, but I didn't even look deeply into it. Don't be like me ... look at every opportunity, think about every opportunity, and ask Him about every opportunity until you understand if it is or isn't for you. Ask yourself if it leads you closer to your highest and greatest or if it's simply a distraction. And ask God the same question ... you'll surely get an answer! He will delight in the question and delight in answering you in the exact way you need Him to!

How do you market your business and faith? What is your belief system in showcasing one over the other and how have you come to peace with your personal solution?

God has never given me the freedom to see the distinction between my business and my faith, and I'm glad He hasn't. They were tied together from the beginning. My faith came first, and the business was an enhancement and encouragement to that faith—just a quicker way to learn to rely on Him. The jobs I held prior to having a business also served as mission fields and became my way of doing life and earning dollars. So it felt natural to see my business as a mission as well. It was an extension of why God put me on this earth. It didn't matter what I did to earn dollars, the purpose was still the same (see the Great Commission in Matthew 28:19–20). Thanks to God's patient nurturing, I've learned to make business a more intentional ministry over the last ten years or so. I would encourage all readers to not separate the message of the business from their faith.

To better communicate that idea, I'd like to share something that happened recently. I attended a funeral a month before writing this chapter. The neighbor who died was described in his eulogy as a "good guy," and that was the way I thought of him too. It made me pause and think; however, what would be said about me? Would I just be the good owner of a good business? Would I be the good guy who was always willing to help? Would I be known as a good husband and father and grandfather who had a really good family? Would I be known for helping my employees and other businesses become good, stable providers? Would I be known as a good Christian? NO! I hope not! That's not good enough! All of those things, though they are good, fall far short of what I want said at my funeral. I am determined to be known for being in a long process of transforming into God's highest and greatest for me while inspiring others to do the same for themselves—but even more than that—I want to be known for being a humble disciple of Christ who unabashedly shared his passion for how much God delights in each person and the wonderful plans He has for each of us to get to our highest and greatest.

My marketing messaging thus far has not had the fish symbol in it, nor is there anything blatant on my company website that would indicate I'm a believer. Often, my first several conversations with an employee, vendor, or potential customer don't reveal that at all. But ... our company motto is "Transforming Lives One Shovel at a Time," and I do promote stories of transformation any way I can get them out there. You likely have your own story of transformation. What I'm promoting is a message of hope, and I like to deliver it with a "hook" so people will want to know more about the author of real transformation.

My company provides paving and pavement maintenance services, which are pretty secular by nature. Everybody likes a smooth, well-maintained road, but the service we provide is not usually life-changing. What is life-changing is the way we treat the people around us, and that starts with the way we see them. We see them as God's creation, and thus they are important! God does not define any of us by our past, and we should not label others that way. We do our best to make each person feel valued.

Caring for people the way God does should be so obvious that people admire it and even say, "Nobody does this for their people; why do you?" When someone asks me "why," they better watch out because there's a gospel presentation coming. I often tell people, "If you're gonna know me, you're gonna hear about God," and then I just tell them some part of my story that, of course, has God's fingerprints all over it. What I put out on social media, say at events or in meetings, or share when I'm speaking publicly always reflects the message on our website and the way we live out our core values. (Which, by the way, are also posted openly.)

God made them, they are important, and He does have a wonderful plan for their lives! That's the message I'm trying to showcase, and it's a message that often creates a positive curiosity—a curiosity that leads them to Jesus!

What wisdom or encouragement would you give to someone who has never blended their faith and business strategy as one? How has it aided in your profitability?

The wording of this question is very interesting to me, in particular, the word *blended*. When I think of a blended family, struggles and difficulties come to mind. But If the members of the family continue to work at it, they eventually, with time and common experience, get mixed together until they are one thing, no matter how imperfect. I also think of a milk-shake or a blended coffee drink from my favorite coffee shop. There are a blend of flavors and ingredients that make up these drinks. But each of the ingredients is still fully present. Even though some of them may get overpowered by stronger flavors, they still can be identified within the mix.

Both faith and business are often large and overpowering concepts, but it doesn't have to be that way. I'm convinced that our faith journey/quest should be the overpowering flavor that is both sweet and savory to our souls and overflowing onto those around us.

Businesses exist to turn a profit and thus supply the needs of those participating in the business. They're also supposed to fund their own growth and provide financial benefit to those that have taken the risk to start and operate them. Faith is similar. It's supposed to profit its owner and be a big part in supplying their needs. It should also serve as an ever present source of hope and, like business, require constant attention and cultivation. And similar to business, it also has a regenerative aspect to it.

The more we invest in it, the more we get out of it. The more we risk being vulnerable with the author of our faith (God) and the people on a similar faith journey, the more we will experience the benefits.

Where the two seemingly diverge is that faith is spiritual and business is worldly and practical. But it's been my experience that, like mixing the blended coffee drink, the greatest flavor and impact will come when the ingredients are mixed. That mixing process of the two things, faith and business, allows for nuances and variety that are world changing. You see, the thing people want most in life is purpose. The word I usually use is *fullness*. If it's fullness we seek, then what we will want most is to operate a highly profitable business that treats its people in an extraordinary way so that their involvement in that business gives them the pathway to that fullness too! Of the hundreds of businesses I've been able to observe, there haven't been any that pulled this off without the owners and highest level managers having a deep connection to their faith. The entrepreneurs that truly "mix" well, love and serve God first and foremost and then love and serve people. Their businesses are noticeably amazing. Sounds easy, right? Nope! It's simple, not easy!

If you're wondering what the first step is to that kind of amazing, purpose-driven business, let me share with you a fool proof method. It'll take some disciplined practice, but it'll work! It'll be worth it! First, talk to God … just talk … and ask Him for the things that you need, like the employees that are a good fit for your business, the right customers for your product, the wisdom needed to make wise decisions, and the vision to touch your community and beyond. James 4:2–3 says, "You do not have because you do not ask." Do this while you're doing the million other things you gotta do every day. And second, read something in His Word every day. The Bible! Every day! This can be short little prayers and a verse or two, but you gotta do it! You'll find a gratefulness and an awareness for others developing in you that you could have only imagined before. After doing these things for decades, I can tell you that there's almost no problem, no matter its complexity, that doesn't have a simple (not necessarily easy) answer that has been addressed in the pages of scripture. These two things create a pathway to finding wisdom and knowing what to do with it.

The question also mentioned profit. Every business needs profit to survive, pivot, and grow. These things are all necessary for any great business, so we as people of faith absolutely can't ignore it. We may not know our exact purpose, but we know we are not on this earth to be mediocre.

But the best thing that happened for my business was when I stepped back three years ago to redefine what I wanted the business to do for me. I had the privilege of doing that with my wife and son who both have been in the business with me for half its life. We all had a stake in what it would provide for us as a reward for our efforts, so we all needed to figure out the "why" behind its existence. Our business had grown tenfold in four years, and we as the owners were all at maximum capacity, due to the rapid growth. The "why" certainly had something to do with profit, but each of us knew it wasn't really about the money.

That's what we all need to figure out for ourselves. "What will the profit provide for us, and how soon do we want it". I hate the term *want*, but that's part of the "desires of our heart" that David and others talk about in the Bible. The better we know the desire of our heart and how close that lines up with God's heart, the closer we can get to knowing how much our business needs to profit and how soon.

I would recommend starting with your personal, nonnegotiable, core values. Then move into the company's core values and quickly into the passion/purpose of the company. Write them down, rework them, and revise them. Make a simple, one-page document you can use for decision making, hiring and firing, and operational standards. Money may be a small part of those things, but we found (and I think you will find) that, although profit may provide opportunity for what we really want, it's not what drives us. For all you faith-driven entrepreneurs, it's about impact and legacy that the profit can help fund.

Closing Thoughts

*Proverbs 16:3 AMP, "Commit your works [and work] to the Lord
[submit and trust them to Him], And your plans will succeed [if you
respond to His will and guidance]."*

What now, you might ask. Commit, submit, and trust. These are action words, but they require practice. I would also suggest that you follow through with these three steps:

1. Make a plan for your faith and business journey. If you're already on one, make an eighteen month plan. Write it all out and remember that situations and conditions will probably change during that eighteen month period, so be prepared to make adjustments according to God's mind and heart. *Ask Him!* Then commit, submit, and trust! If you have yet to start a plan, then mark a date on the calendar that you will begin, officially. You will have a number of tasks to do to get ready for your start-up before you get to that date on the calendar. *Ask Him* His mind and heart on the details of what He's asked you to do…. He will answer through a book, a program, or a person, and when He does, you just commit, submit, and trust. And remember that the plan and maybe even the date may change, but *keep asking Him!*
2. Treat the people on the journey with you incredibly well. Remember the golden rule and prioritize relationships! That is what will make your plans succeed!
3. Feed on His Word every day because the answers to all of life's problems are there!

And always ask Him!

You serve me a six-course dinner right in front of my enemies. You revive my drooping head; my cup brims with blessing. Your beauty and love chase after me every day of my life. I'm back home in the house of GOD for the rest of my life

Psalm 23: 5–6.

Alejandra Crisafulli

AWARDING WINNING MASTER LIFE COACH AND GLOBAL SPEAKER.

With over twenty years of experience in coaching, training, and development, Alejandra is considered one of the "pioneers" of the coaching industry. She has worked with over 5,000 coaching clients, trained over 300 coaches, guided entrepreneurs to scale into multi 6+-figure and 7+-figure businesses, trained and developed multiple C-suite executives, and has built a multimillion dollar coffee business with her husband, Eric, that spans Southern California. Known for her engaging and compelling style, she has taken practical business expertise and married it to energetic spiritual science, giving her clients the modern-day magic that gets results without the BS.

Chapter 4
The Only Answer to Self Help

Would you describe your entrepreneurial adventure as a solution, a sign, or a wonder based on my personal testimony and experience?

For the past twenty years of my life, I have been helping people— helping them overcome blocks in their lives, overcome obstacles in their relationships, overcome fear in all areas of their lives, and overcome cycles of pain and trauma being repeated again and again. And yet, here I found myself in the most precarious of positions. Me, Alejandra, award winning master life coach, was lying in a hospital bed suffering from a panic attack.

The bright fluorescent lights and the beep, beep, beeping of the heart monitor only sent me further into questioning how I got here and what was going on? Little did I know this would be the beginning of a year-long journey to unravel everything I thought I knew. My entire life was about to change and my business as well.

I have been a master life coach for over twenty years and have seen thousands of clients transform their lives through our work together. But I always felt like there was something missing. I know now there *was* someone missing. I was mindlessly walking through life and business, doing what I had always done or listening to what others told me I should be doing. Never once did I think I was on the wrong path. I was successful but only to a degree. I had a good life, but it was dull and complacent.

Many people would have looked from the outside and thought I had it all together. And why not? From the outside, I was doing the work I loved and helping people. But I was helping them from a very limited self-reliant, self-improvement, self-development perspective, admittedly a self-sufficient, egotistical place.

After leaving that hospital, I went through one of the darkest times of my life. I had no idea how crappy a person could feel until then. I had always heard it from clients, but going through it myself elevated it to quite another level. I remember someone asking what it felt like. Here is the best way I can describe it—my soul felt sick. And it was. I realized that I had been missing the most significant piece of my life, but my work and business were missing this piece as well—God.

I met God that year. It wasn't a moment of divine intervention; it was a process of Him pulling me out of the darkness and saying, "Enough! You are mine, and we have work to do!" I had to unlearn what I had taught for nearly fifteen years and rebuild on the foundation of Him, His work, and His doing ... Not mine.

I had delivered something powerful in my work without Him. But with Him, my life and work took a 180 degree turn that set everything I did on a foundation that creates long-lasting healing. While He blessed me with the basis of a successful business before I gave my life to Him, I couldn't grow it to the level of success I had originally envisioned. But once I became a follower of Christ, the 180 method was born and became the **Solution** to bringing **Him** back into traditional self-help models.

My entrepreneurial adventure has been a conjecture of all sorts of experiences, lessons, and hardships, but I am where I am today because of my reformed relationship with God. It was through my testimony that not only I was reborn but my business as well. Therefore, my success as an entrepreneur and my uncovering of various methods and programs that have helped people become their true selves and fulfill their life's purpose in alignment with God are a side effect of His wondrous personal work in my life—work that required a significant breakdown and led to a flourishing and prosperous breakthrough to make my business what is today.

What Christ-like solutions have you discovered that make your day-to-day business manageable?

The demands of running a business are a very taxing reality. We wear multiple hats and are constantly made to feel like we're being pulled in every direction. From my experience, the rapid switches from coach to sales associate to marketing strategist to financial reporter to customer service and everything in between stretched me so thin I couldn't relax through my responsibilities and find joy in my work. I was "dealing." Dealing is a term I use throughout my coaching method because it perfectly encapsulates how most people live their lives. People often believe they have a manageable equilibrium between pain and pleasure. Yet this "balance" is really just a battle for control, and we hold onto this attempt at control for dear life. In truth, this fight to maintain balance is only a surface-level solution to the overwhelming facets of human existence. I would like to know what Jesus thought of me as He watched me trudge through my days, looking for some sanity while I perpetually tried to control and manage my way through every task. I imagine He would react like this: "Alejandra, you don't need to make everything so hard. Simply give it to me."

I know that the gifts of the Spirit and my God-given purpose as a coach have gotten me to my level of success. Coaching is at the core of my work; It is where I thrive. However, at one point in my career, I was overwhelmed. I was seeing seven to eight clients a day, which allowed no time for myself or for Him. I couldn't handle the workload, and one more email would be enough to push me over the edge. I couldn't do it anymore and just broke down. I needed to surrender completely and 180 myself and my business.

The two leading Christ-like solutions that directionally shifted my day-to-day to create a more manageable existence for me were to identify the "why" and to trust. Let's talk about the first one. I know that many educational business resources out there tell you to find your "why." But I do not provide traditional self-help resources for uncovering solutions.

These solutions are often temporary, and you find yourself 360'd at exactly where you began—once again overwhelmed and flailing for some semblance of grounded-ness. What I want for myself and my clients is to 180 our directional healing, and the only way to achieve this is to find our "why" centered in Christ.

When thinking about their "why," most people are drawn to a human-based desire; this is usually driven by ego or, as I like to tell my clients, E.G.O (Edging God Out). Their reason for going on and pushing through the challenges are external and earthly-based motivators, things that are not rooted in spiritual, God-centered "whys." The essential motivator for pushing through the complex parts of business is returning to the core mission, which is for the sake of building His kingdom and His glory, not our own. I had to remove the layers and all the hats I was trying to control and genuinely surrender my own wants and desires to Him in order to uncover my Christ-like "why." Here it is, my mission and my divine purpose: Help bring people closer to God.

As for the second solution … release the control. This raises the question of how one releases control. And the answer is only through trust and surrender. We tend to separate trust from surrender, but they go hand-in-hand, and here is the critical part of understanding—surrender is the action, and trust is the result. People talk about trust as a separate thing you do, but it's not. The action of surrender naturally ends in trust. All the hats that I had been wearing and all the dealing was for the sake of control, and that control was rooted in my inability to trust. I felt that, If I were not in charge, I would not be successful. But this is where the surrendering took place, and that is when God showed up in my business doing the work with me. Consider the phrase *surrendering it up to God*. You may think that surrendering is a one-and-done, but, if you notice the language, the I-N-G makes it active and present. When I actively practice surrendering every day, trust occurs. The result is an ease and a return to my purpose of bringing my clients into the light and helping them come closer to God. In the spirit of these core values, I am able to manage my business day-to-day.

What signs have been given to you along the way that have led you to say yes to exploring and activating your entrepreneurial spirit?

All entrepreneurs start their businesses with a vision—a dream, a desire to start something great. When that prompting comes from God, an entrepreneur's passion for fulfilling their aspirations grows even stronger. This vision is the easy part. Bringing goals and dreams into fruition is where the challenge of entrepreneurship truly lies.

As my business began to take off and I started to build my success and see my vision come to life, I knew I was ready for the next step. I wanted to create something big but needed the space in which to do so. I had created my successful vocation while in a small extra office space in my house. But I knew It was time to take this step, I knew I was ready. I decided to lease an office space where I could hold workshops. However, standing in the workshop space, a clipboard and pen extended towards me, I was frozen, struggling to proceed and overcome by fear and doubts. I heard that voice in my head telling me that I wasn't ready more than I heard I wasn't worthy.

I didn't know God at the time, but, if I had, I would have been on my knees praying for guidance. The wonderful reality of the Lord is that He is with you whether you know Him or not. He was with me that day. I signed the papers despite my fear, and as soon as my landlord left me to my new space, I fell to the floor and cried. You know, like the ugly cry, crying for all that I had gone through, all that was to come, and all the questions surrounding "what am I doing?" In an attempt to calm myself down and find some solace, I did all I could think to do, walk.

I didn't know where I was going, I just needed some air, some reprieve from my overwhelming worry. My office was in this nice coastal neighborhood that had all these expensive and beautiful homes, and I kept admiring them as I walked. I began to express my apprehension out loud. "What am I supposed to do now?" I asked. As that question took on various forms and my feet kept pushing me forward, the oddest thing happened. I looked over and saw a taxi cab. For a taxi cab to be in this type of neighborhood was enough to catch my attention, but the thing that stopped me in my tracks was the sign above the taxi. Lit up in bright white with black letters was one word—COACH. Where have you ever seen a taxi cab with a lighted sign that says *coach*?

You know those instances when you realize something was so easy, and this relief washes over you, and you begin to laugh? Well, that was my moment—instant relief and laughter. Coach … that was my answer. All I had to do was coach. This sign was the first of many that would come along to direct my path to finding God and having a deeply intimate relationship with Jesus. All I had to do was coach, and the rest would unfold.

The power of my entrepreneurial spirit lies in my ability to urge, inspire, and train people to heal, not just deal. When the doubts and fears come in to hold me back from pursuing my visions, I am reminded that activating the power of my entrepreneurial spirit lies in the gifts God has given me. The sign to coach and lead as I always have will motivate me to push past the setbacks and fears.

How is "wonder" a part of your rhythm as a leader, visionary, and business builder?

I always knew I was going to be a ballet dancer. From the first time I entered a dark stage and felt the adrenaline pump through my body, the hot lights blinding me, and the fluidity and precision of my muscles guiding me through my routines, there was no doubt, no pain, just me, the audience, and my unmatched passion for performing. I knew this passion would burn in me forever, and I was prepared to dedicate my life to keeping it alive. I belonged on a stage. Turns out God had a very different plan.

I was in a car accident at seventeen and tore ligaments in my back. Just like that, my future in ballet died, along with my spirit and passion. The loss of ballet felt like the loss of myself—my identity and my purpose. I had never paid attention to academics because I knew I was going to be a dancer. Why even bother with anything else? I had many people throughout my life ask, "What if you get injured and can't dance anymore. Then what?" I found this question cynical and paranoid. That would never happen to me—until it did—and all I had left of my dreams were devastation, pain, and most of all anger … anger at the situation, at myself, and at what had been taken from me. The anger led me to be rebellious through drugs, alcohol, and an abusive relationship, which ultimately resulted in me becoming a single mom. But God will always use our mistakes to lead us back to Him. He took what I thought was the end of my life and turned it into the beginning.

Choosing to be a single mother, I knew I had to straighten up my act. So I focused on the skills that I did have. I always had this very strong ability to lead others. Leadership was the gift that led me into entrepreneurship. Eventually, I became a life coach and built a successful multimillion dollar business.

During my training as a coach, I was introduced to public speaking. I had a mentor once tell me that I had a knack for connecting and engaging others and that I should run with that. For my first speaking engagement, I walked out onto the stage, took my position in the darkness, and then the lights came on, bright and shining. I found myself right back where I had started my journey—on stage. But this time it was for God's will and purpose, not my own. I often wonder about His plans for me and my business, but my story and testimony act as evidence to the miracle that is the unknown. Now I am conscious to remain curious and obedient to God's will for my life because of this wonder.

Who biblically has been a consistent mentor in your pursuit of excellence as an entrepreneur? What are their unique character traits, and how have they modeled being a joy-full entrepreneur well?

The most consistent biblical mentor in my life has been Paul. My first encounter with the apostle was about four years ago while sitting in my church cafe across from a pastor. To be at church was a new sensation in itself, but to be at church across from one of the lead pastors was completely foreign. In an attempt to continue my pursuit of God, I agreed to meet with Pastor Bryan and talk to him about my testimony. I wasn't sure what his intention was, but I was so voraciously hungry to know God and wanted more from what I was experiencing in my new faith journey, so I agreed to coffee. He asked me what my life purpose was. Before the health issues I had faced, which brought me to God, I would have had a clear answer, but now I wasn't so sure. His question left me stunned, and in my silence brewed a longing. My life's purpose used to be clear and defined. I was ambitious, intense, and determined within my business, doing what I thought was helping people. Those traits were admirable, yes, but they were misplaced. I attributed the fruits of success to my accomplishments—accomplishments that were out of alignment with God's kingdom. As I fumbled my way into trying to answer his question, he took a deep breath and looked me in the eyes and said, "You remind me so much of Paul." What? "Paul who?" was my first thought, as I'd never really known who Paul was other than as an apostle. How Bryan could see anything remotely similar in us was beyond me. But I see it now.

Paul believed so profoundly in his work before he met Jesus and thought he was doing good in the world. But it wasn't until he was brought to his knees and condemned for his persecution of the Lord that he realized just how wrong he had been. In his literal "come to Jesus" moment, he discovered how the gifts God had given him were not being used correctly. Through his breakdown, he discovered his true purpose. With God as his new foundation, he used the talents that he always possessed and redirected them in collaboration with the Lord.

His purpose … bring people closer to God. And that is what I know my purpose to be today. He inspires the true essence of joy-filled entrepreneurship. Because no matter if business is good or bad, there is still joy, free from the circumstances.

What wisdom or encouragement would you give someone who has never blended their faith and business strategy as one? How has it aided in your profitability?

After coming to faith, I had a decision to make. How could I possibly change everything in my business that I had done for decades to now include the truth of God?

I agonized over this question for months, in complete conflict with my ego. All of my business knowledge and acumen were rooted in metaphysical sciences and not the truth of God. I knew I couldn't surrender my life to the Lord and keep my business separate. So I had to make a decision. The funny thing about decisions is that they are different from choices. Choices you can change; there is a flexibility to them. But to decide is to permanently kill off every other choice.

There were so many changed lives due to what I had taught and what I had built. Now I was going to change the basis of my entire career—tear it down and rebuild on the Lord's firm foundation. I didn't know where to even begin. My newly appointed Christian mentor, Laura, supported me throughout the process of transitioning my business. She helped me to solidify my decision to shift my brand and take the leap of faith. I leapt off the cliff trusting that, together with God, I would grow my wings on the way down.

It was not an overnight shift. A 180 doesn't always happen overnight. It was a slow-burn shift that built momentum to become what my business is today. Looking back now, it's silly to me that I even questioned shifting my business to be a God-centered pursuit. The changes in my success and the success of my clients have been drastic. I used to worry incessantly about where my next client would come from. And I was forever seeking to find the next big thing, be that a client, speaking event, or networking opportunity. Coming across a less profitable season of clients and work would leave me feeling deeply dejected and frustrated. Everything is different now.

I don't have to push anymore for clients. If someone says no, which is the rarity now, I don't go down a spiraling path of self-pity. It lights me up knowing that I trust Him to bring me whom I am meant to work with and help guide. My bottom line is three times what it was before, but the more important part is that I am using the gifts which God had designed and intended for me to use. It is for His purpose, not my own. When you 180 your business to be in alignment with Him, claiming Him and inviting Him into your business, there is an overflow of protection and blessing.

> *You prepare a table before me in the presence of my enemies. You anoint my head with oil; my cup OVERFLOWS (Psalm 23:5).*

Closing Thoughts

Did you know that you are in a relationship with your business? We often look at relationships strictly between people, but the truth is we are in relationships with all things. We have relationships with time, money, and, yes, business. I had always known this, but I needed help in order to have a healthy relationship with my business. Having been a life coach in the self-help industry for over twenty years, fifteen of them without knowing God, I now understand why I could never truly experience a healthy relationship with my business. There was a hole, an emptiness within me that I kept trying to fill by using my business. However, just like any other relationship that you try to use for this purpose, it just leaves you empty and wanting more—the 360 effect. God healed this, and now, instead of looking at my business as a part of my identity, I see it as a part of my purpose. A purpose that I fulfill in conjunction with the Lord.

Ask and it shall be given to you; seek and you will find; knock and the door will be opened to you

Matthew 7:7.

Sharon Davenport

Sharon, a.k.a. the Happy Highlighter, and her family live in the horse and bourbon capital of the world, Lexington, Kentucky. As a Licensed Massage Therapist and a Nationally Approved Provider for Continuing Education, Sharon has been "unofficially" coaching clients since 2005. Now, as a Certified Life and Career Coach and health and personal growth and development nerd, Sharon founded ActivateU, where she promotes holistic wellness, mindset mastery, and Holy-Spirit connection through her Wholeness Principle.

Known for her SuperPower of collaboration, Sharon's connections with some of today's best known influencers in the personal growth industry have given her a unique perspective on how to help people pivot their mindset and level up their lives. This shift in perspective often leads people to finding freedom and success in the key areas of life and business. Tune into the *What's Your SuperPower?* podcast as Sharon interviews some of these amazing individuals. As the Happy Highlighter, Sharon desires to help ActivateU into who you are created to be.

Authentically caring about other people's best interests has helped Sharon succeed in the area of sales and is how she founded Integrity Enterprises, which has helped coaching & wellness companies transform lives and close millions in sales since 2020. Passion, not pushy, is how she helps ActivateU and others too!

Chapter 5
Wisdom from a Wonder Seeker

Would you describe your entrepreneurial adventure as a solution, a sign, or a wonder based on your personal testimony and experience? Explain.

Don't you just love it when you get asked a question that tries to put you in a box? It drives those of us that tend toward being "rule followers" a bit crazy, as my first inclination was to pick one of the options above, but, alas, my entrepreneurial adventure has been all of the above: a solution, a sign, and a wonder, for sure! For instance, have you ever experienced that deep knowing that you were meant for more? Have you ever had that burning desire to explore the world or maybe just felt like you didn't quite belong in the regular "mold" of life? Yeah, me too. Well, "HERE'S YOUR SIGN" that you may have been born with the entrepreneurial spirit also, my friend!

Lord knows I was, and it took God bonking me over the head with MY SIGN a few times for me to finally kick fear in the face and step out into this wild world of wonder! Wonder-full it is, too, most of the time.... Speaking of wonder, it has been a joy and a wonder to be able to work from home and travel to incredible locations, like where I am currently writing this from—Egypt!! Yes, Egypt! I am presently gazing at the Red Sea after spending time floating in it with my family for most of the day. I am loving this entrepreneurial adventure and all the wonders it presents, not to mention the people I have had the privilege to meet and the life-long connections we have made along this journey as well.

How has this adventure been a solution, you may ask? Well, I'm glad you did, as it has been the solution to knowing I wasn't made for the "normal" nine to five mold or sitting in an office all day—a solution for the simple fact that I won't look back at the end of my life and say, "I wish I had …" or "What if …?" I haven't just said that one day I will do that. Instead, this realization about myself has opened doors to opportunities many people just dream about or hope will happen to them one day. You, too, my friend, can learn to recognize the signs, enjoy the wonder, and discover the solutions of the entrepreneurial adventure, if you desire! Sometimes it just requires taking the first step. So what do you say? Are you ready to experience all the incredible things this life has to offer? Great! First step, get on your knees and pray, then get on your feet and take action! What? Not that easy, you say? Then do yourself a huge favor, and invest in yourself by hiring a coach. Not sure where to find a good one? Reach out to me; I know a few who love Jesus and will help Activate U into who God has called you to be!

What Christ-like solutions have you discovered that make your day-to-day business manageable and fruitful?

My incredible husband has a saying: "There are no problems, just solutions." What if we took on each and every day with that in mind? How would that help you?

Now hear me out. While it is definitely the path for me, the entrepreneurial life is not for everyone, as it has a certain level of uncertainty that can be hard on the whole family at times. One of the Christ-like solutions we have discovered that makes our day-to-day business manageable and fruitful is having open communication with those closest to us. I am beyond grateful that my husband and I are on the same page as we pursue this adventure together, supporting one another and understanding it takes a certain level of freedom and trust to be profitable in this pursuit.

It also helps that we have always communicated well, and we are each other's biggest fans. Having the right people on this journey can make the biggest difference, especially because they can be part of the solution equation as well as your support system. You don't need a lot of people in your corner, just a few key players. You don't have those people, you say? Then go find them! Put yourself in the room with people you want to be like, and never be afraid to be the least talented one in the room. That's how you will grow!

While there are tons of books out there—many of which I have read—on starting your morning out right, they leave out the most important thing: giving this day back to the One who created it! Besides having the right people in my corner, starting the day with prayer and gratitude (along with dedicating each day, with all its uncertainties, to the Lord) has been key for me. When I give each day to Him and surrender it all from the start, it helps me navigate the unexpected detours so much better! Start doing this, and see what happens for you. A simple way to do this, which I heard from an older pastor, is to say, "Good Morning, Lord! What would You have me do today? My life is Yours; my time is Yours. I give myself to You; guide me today, Lord. I wish to do the things You desire me to do. I'm Yours to command. Amen." I'd love to hear how things positively change for you as you put this into practice daily too!

Other great tools include time-blocking the day, using the Focus Keeper App to stay on track, and not getting too bent out of shape when unexpected disturbances come up, as they always do. Making sure to have an end time to my day so I can spend time with my family is key for me as well. I could write a whole book on this topic but will leave it here for now.

What signs have been given to you along the way that have led you to say yes to exploring and activating your entrepreneurial spirit?

As we are currently in transition from Hurghada, Egypt, where we spent a few days on the Red Sea, to Luxor, where we will board our Nile cruise, I am overwhelmed with a sense of gratitude. To be spending this time with my husband, son, and our extended family in a country I grew up reading about in the Bible is such a gift! What better place to write to you about signs and wonders than from where some spectacular signs were given to those I grew up reading about, right?! As a reminder or if you are new to the Bible—such a good read, by the way—the wise men were given the North Star as a sign to find the Messiah. Mary and Joseph took baby Jesus and fled to Egypt when Joseph was warned in a dream about Harrod's plan to kill all the baby boys under the age of two. Then there is the story of how Joseph was sold into slavery by his brothers and how God elevated him in Egypt and used him to save his family and the chosen people during the famine. This is one of my favorite stories in the Bible; go reread it! Well, after you finish this book, of course. ... One other important story that took place in Egypt is the story of Moses. Man! How cool to be walking the same sands so many thousands of years later!

You are probably wondering how these stories relate to my entrepreneurial activation. I believe in signs, wonders, and the truth that miracles still happen today, just as they did in the Bible. In fact, I don't just believe it, I know it to be true, as I have firsthand experience. Besides some of my own personal experiences, I grew up with a powerful prayer-warrior Grandma. I loved hearing her stories about how God would wake her up in the middle of the night to pray for some friends on the mission field, only to find out months later that at that exact time and day, her friends were surrounded by adversaries who miraculously stopped their advances. Later, these same adversaries would come to the missionaries and tell them that they saw many more people in the camp than they thought were there, so they retreated instead of robbing them or possibly worse. Her friends referred to these protectors as angels who showed up when my Grandmother, who was on the other side of the world, awoke to pray for them. You see, when we are open to it, God activates His people to awaken and miracles happen!

Then there was the time when my dad was about twelve years old and was playing outside in the hot Florida sun with his cousins. He was racing one of his cousins to a tree and didn't see the rattlesnake until he was already upon it. Thinking quickly, he threw an arm back to stop his cousin while his momentum continued to propel him forward. He lifted his leg to push back on the base of the tree just as the rattlesnake lashed out. My dad said it was the craziest thing ... as his leg was pushing off the base of the tree and the rattlesnake was in full-strike mode, the snake froze in mid strike. Though my dad should have been impaled by the poisonous teeth, the snake was literally frozen in midair! As he fell away from the tree, he looked back to see the snake slithering off. He ran as fast as he could to share with his mom, but when he burst through the door to the house screaming, "MOM!!!" she held up her hand to quiet him and said, "I know ..." She then proceeded to tell him how she had seen it all in a vision from God and had immediately hit her knees in prayer. She then told my dad what he didn't see. He didn't see the angel that had grabbed the snake mid strike, making it seem like it was frozen when, in fact, it had been stopped by the power of prayer.

Oh, my friends, I have several of these supernatural true stories, like the time the hurricane split when my Grandma told it to in the name of Jesus and the time God protected me from a bad crash one foggy morning on back country roads as I rushed to school. Alas, you will have to read my personal book to hear more!

How do you allow supernatural signs to direct your path, process, profit plan, and partnerships in business?

With all of the incredible true testimonies I just shared in the last section, how could I not ask Jesus to direct my path, processes, and profit plan in business and partnerships? Well, to get real with you, even with these signs and others I have experienced, I still have my moments of doubt. During these moments, I don't necessarily doubt what God can do, but, instead, I question what I can achieve and my own self-worth. Ever been there? Funny isn't it—that as a life and career coach, I help people see their worth and value all the time yet have struggled with my own worth? But God (I love that phrase!) has used my personal struggle in this area to lead me to invest in myself more, which has opened more doors and created more opportunities! Do I still struggle with self-worth? Sometimes, yes. But I know my value and worth is not found here on Earth, and the only one I truly desire to please is my heavenly Father. Staying kingdom-focused helps when making decisions in all of these areas.

Being a licensed massage therapist for over eighteen years has also led me to pay attention to the many different signs that arise in my own life and body and in the lives and bodies of others as well. And because Jesus said He needed to leave His disciples so someone greater than He could dwell with us (the Holy Spirit), a prayer of mine is to be led by the Holy Spirit daily. So how does one hear from the Holy Spirit? Through the years, I have learned to pay attention to the physical manifestations of emotions in my body when dealing with decisions, business, and profit plans. Although prayer is key and my first plan of action, I also tune in to how I feel in my gut and chest. I have learned to pay attention to these physical signs when dealing with decisions. Okay, I know what you may be thinking now; this gal just got weird, right? None of that woo woo stuff Sharon …

All right, listen. I am a very logical and analytical woman. Just ask my husband, and he will tell you; he's the more emotional one in our relationship, and I love him for it. Due to my rational nature, it has been an honor and a privilege to study and understand the body and world of massage through a more scientific lens. So let's stay grounded as you explore this with me for a moment. Think about experiencing butterflies in your stomach or doing something you know is not right and feeling sick to your stomach. These are both physical manifestations of emotions. When we actually pay attention to how we react and, yes, how we feel in our processes, plans, partnerships, and business dealings and pair that with prayer, I believe it is a beautiful way in which the Holy Spirit can be experienced in our lives on a whole different level. Want to dig deeper? Reach out to me personally, or read my forthcoming book!

How is "wonder" a part of your rhythm as a leader, visionary, and business builder?

If we just stop long enough to recognize it, there is a little wonder present in the everyday race of life. What's the point of building a business if we don't have a little wonder wrapped up in it too?

In getting to know me, you might actually say I am a "wonder" seeker. Maybe this is where my love for travel and exploration comes from as well as my desire to see lives transformed and people realize their God-given potential. Witnessing these spectacular wonders keeps the fire inside me lit! Walking with someone as they experience a breakthrough, see Jesus in a way they never have before, heal from past wounds, or step into their calling is a magnificent wonder to behold. This is where having a coach can help you see the vision for your life when things may have gotten cloudy for you, and helping to clear the clouds, encourages us coaches and leaders to keep getting up in the morning too!

How has your faith been sharpened as an entrepreneur?

With uncertainty as a constant in the life of an entrepreneur (and if I don't want anxiety and overwhelm to rule my life), I have to continually surrender and trust in the Lord. Maybe I'm just speaking for myself, but, in my experience, most entrepreneurs like a certain level of *control!* Giving up control takes faith and requires daily surrender and releasing it all to Him.

No, I am not saying this makes everything miraculously work out and that I don't have to do my share of work; I'm saying **surrender and release** have brought joy back into my entrepreneurial adventure and make the ups and downs more manageable. God is in control, and I can remind Him that this is His business, and He's got the wheel. As a result, I get to trust Him to steer us in the right direction!

What wisdom or encouragement would you give someone who has never blended their faith and business strategy as one? How has it aided in your profitability?

Try it. What would it profit a man to gain the whole world yet lose his soul (Mark 8:36)? Nothing. When we keep our eyes on Jesus and continually surrender our business to Him, it may not look like we imagined it would, but it will be better than we ever imagined. It also relieves the level of stress and brings a sense of peace as we release control to our creator. Invite Jesus into your business books, pay your tithes, give generously, and watch how He expands your territory! We have seen the fruits; you can too!

Closing Thoughts

Miracles, signs, and wonders happen around us every single day. Just like in the verse at the beginning of this chapter, the more I pray and **Ask** the Lord, the more I **Seek** His wisdom, and the more I take action and **Knock, the** more signs and wonders I experience. Our precious time here on Earth is limited, and there are big and small wonders to be experienced and enjoyed every day. It is my hope for you as you continue along your journey that you seek first the kingdom of God, and then collaborate with those who also authentically follow Him. My prayer for you is that the Lord will glorify His name in your life, that you will experience the Holy Spirit like never before, and that you will see miracles, signs, and wonders in your life so you know beyond a shadow of doubt how much Jesus loves you and that we are here for so much more than what we might possibly imagine. Remember, it is not about us; it's about surrender and service. And through this, we will experience more joy and wonder than we ever thought possible. It's been an honor to have you read my chapter. If it touched your heart in some way, feel free to reach out to me on Instagram: sharondavenport_ or email me at Sharon@ActivateU7.com.

Keep this Book of the Law always on your lips; meditate on it day and night, so that you may be careful to do everything written in it. Then you will be prosperous and successful

Joshua 1:8.

Marcus Ellis

As a devout man of Christ, a dedicated husband, a father of five beautiful children, and a performer called to use the gift of his voice for more than music, Marcus' life has been transformed by fully surrendering to God.

Performing professionally as a lead vocalist in rock and funk bands across the Southeast for over twenty-five years, Marcus is now the lead vocalist for White Tie Rock Ensemble, a world-renowned Classic Rock tribute band. Recently, in the late stages of his singing career, he prayed to heal his voice and received a download from God in the form of a calling. The calling is to remain on the big stage and use his voice not only to sing but to speak and to ease the world's suffering by becoming a "Spreader of Love."

His mission is to share God's splendor through a simple question and answer—"Hey! Guess What? I Love You"—one random stranger at a time. He prays to make an impact on others by simply being a conduit of God's grace and love.

Chapter 6
Leap of Faith

Would you describe your entrepreneurial adventure as a solution, a sign, or a wonder based on your personal testimony and experience? Explain.

Hey! Guess what? I Love You!

I would 100 percent describe my business as a solution! I'm so overjoyed to write that sentence! I've always desired to help people in life and in the businesses that I chose to work for. A few verses of scripture immediately come to mind before I explain the heart posture of wanting to help people and not hurt them. Proverbs 11:25 says, "A generous person will prosper; whoever refreshes others will be refreshed." Next, are Jesus' words in Matthew, which many know as "The Golden Rule." "So in everything, do to others what you would have them do to you, for this sums up the Law and the Prophets" (Matthew 7:12). And then there is a very important verse Jesus spoke in Mark 8:36 that says, "What good is it for someone to gain the whole world, yet forfeit their soul?" These verses are so rich! I cherish their guidance and take them to heart and action. With that said, we must "do" them; we must put His Word into action—not just ruminate, recite, and recall.

There are multitudes upon multitudes of businesses out there where one can "get rich" while the business of choice harms people, instead of helping them. Here's where that heart posture comes into play. I have friends that are bar owners who encouraged me to open a bar. "The money is great, and you get to have a good time while making an amazing living!" they said. Being a musician, my old self was often out late at night performing, and I often saw how much fun (at the time) my bar-owner friends were having … until someone got hurt. Seeing the harm that resulted from these lucrative, money-making businesses really struck a chord with me. It chilled me to my core. I became more and more aware of other businesses (which I won't name) that harmed people, all in the name of the almighty dollar bill.

My grandfather once told me that I better know exactly what I wanted to do in my business life by the time I was thirty years of age, or I'd be in big trouble. I told him that I already knew what I wanted to do and that was to be a musician. I can still see his head slowly bowing as it shook from side to side. Poor guy …

I went on to spend nearly thirty years in the pro audio, video, and lighting industry. MUSIC! I worked directly with houses of worship, school districts, stadiums, and arenas across our beautiful country. I felt great pride about the systems I designed and sold because I knew that the vast majority of them were broadcasting God's Word on a consistent basis. I mean, how wonderful is that? How many beautiful souls were inspired and drawn closer to God by His message being broadcast through the sound, video, and lighting systems that my colleagues and I created and provided?

If you know me or get to know me (which I greatly encourage), you'll quickly realize that I am what I usually refer to myself as, "the freak in the room." I mean that with the greatest of positivity and love. I'm not your average, run-of-the-mill type of guy. I tend to "swim upstream" or "cut against the grain," so to speak. Well, the company that I worked for was bought out by a large corporation. Suddenly, I went from working for a "Mom & Pop" to a megacorp. Not my jam! Being a cog in the wheel of "Corporate America" was the last thing that I wanted to be a part of or align myself with. I felt that strongly, even from an early age. That's the reason I got into the music business in the first place! Not that there's anything wrong with working for a large corporation, if that's what you do, and that's your thing. It's just not for me, and it doesn't fit my way of living and being. So one day I looked around, and I realized that that's exactly where I was—even though I was in the music business. I became frustrated and upset with myself and couldn't shake the feeling. So I began to investigate options and explore ways to make a move.

Fast-forward to the Covid scene. As we all are acutely aware, the season of Covid changed lives on a monumental scale—the Big Reset as we call it. Those who were fortunate enough not to be affected by the virus began to realize that this was the time to make a drastic life change, and I did just that. I became a real estate investor. Why, you may ask—because it's such an honor and a joy to assist people in need! Being a solution provider is immensely fulfilling in multiple ways! I work closely with homeowners who are in stressful and sometimes painful situations, and that's putting it mildly. I primarily work with folks who are in the foreclosure process. If the homeowner desires to keep their house, I make every effort and work every angle to fight the banks on their behalf to negotiate a solution that benefits them. Unfortunately, the owners retaining their house is a rare occasion. Usually, people are tired, worn out, and exhausted from the situation and simply desire to move on. I then assess their home and give them a cash offer that will allow them to pay off their mortgage as well as have some money left over for moving expenses and a down payment on their next home. If the seller and I aren't crying happy tears of joy, hugging, and telling each other, "I love you!" when all is said and done, then it's not a deal for me or them! If I need to convince, coerce, or talk someone into selling their home, then it's not a deal! I pray daily that God shows me who to serve that day. You'd be amazed at how He answers that prayer each and every day! I also pray that He only shows me people who need my assistance and expertise in my business. Show me those who need grace, compassion, and kindness! What a joy! By praying that over my daily life and my business, I'm at peace knowing that I am serving God and His children. People over profit! I don't focus on the money. The money will come as long as I am Jesus-minded and walking the path that God has laid out for me. With that said, I do pray for the provision to come.

What Christ-like solutions have you discovered that make your day-to-day business manageable and fruitful?

I discovered and am learning that prayer is my sword, my solution. As I mentioned previously, each morning in my moment of prayer, I ask God to show me who to serve, in whatever capacity that may be—whether it is telling a stranger, "I love you!" as God puts it on my heart, offering a homeless person clothing, food, etc., or serving someone in my business. As Tamra Andress says, "It's *all* God's business."

Something that took me a lifetime to figure out is that our hardships and challenges can be learned from. Jesus taught us to love one another, no matter what the circumstance. In business, we all come across people that we don't necessarily jive with, or, frankly, don't like. Through reading the red words in the Bible, I've learned that we are all God's children and that we all have something beautifully positive to offer. My struggles are my story! The tests are my testimony! My mess is my message! There is a teachable moment in all things … especially in our toughest times!

My favorite Bible verse in this season can be found in the Book of James. It says, "Consider it pure joy, my brothers and sisters, whenever you face trials of many kinds, because you know that the testing of your faith produces perseverance. Let perseverance finish its work so that you may be mature and complete, not lacking anything" (James 1:2–4).

God uses us and our struggles to light the path for others. There's a reason you're going through your mess, Baby! Your mission, after your trials and tribulations, is to share your story with others in His awesome name! Deploying this heart posture has not only grown my business but made it easier to deal with my day-to-day life with Him.

Recently, I knocked on the door of a house belonging to a beautiful soul. Her home was in the process of foreclosure, and she was at risk of losing it to the bank. I had prayed earlier that morning for God to point out who I needed to serve with His guidance. I don't know why I am always blown away when God answers my prayers, and this experience was no different. This nice lady was weeks away from losing her house not because she wasn't making her payments but because the insurance company had canceled her homeowner's policy, due to the age of her roof. As a result of her policy being canceled, the bank stopped cashing her mortgage payment checks without notice! Can you imagine? She didn't have the funds to fix her roof as well as make her mortgage payment. She had also been caring for her adult daughter who suffered from mental illness, and the cost associated with her daughter's care was massive.

We must've talked on her porch for an hour. We negotiated a deal that would serve her as well as provide for my family. She was so thankful! As I was leaving, she told me, "I am so grateful that you knocked on my door today! This was a God thing! I was just going to let the bank take my home and get an apartment." Folks, the money she will receive will pay off her mortgage and get her into a nice apartment. Not only is God allowing me to serve her in that capacity, but He also had me driving her around town to help her find an apartment as well as other tasks that will assist her at the property until the deal closes. I drove away from that meeting laughing with tears in my eyes. Out loud I exclaimed, "Thank you Lord for answering my prayer and allowing me to serve you and your child!"

Whoever is kind to the poor lends to the LORD, and he will reward them for what they have done. (Proverbs 19:17).

What signs have been given to you along the way that have led you to say yes to exploring and activating your entrepreneurial spirit?

I love the small, simple signs from God. I also love to pray during my early morning walks and runs. There's nothing like talking to God as the sun is rising over Pensacola Bay, let me tell ya! During these moments, God often sends me signs using majestic birds. More times than I can count, God sends me a bird sign just as I'm finishing a line of a prayer. He usually sends me hawks in these moments. I love that! Sometimes they scream as they fly overhead. Out of nowhere, they soar right past me as an acknowledgment from Him. "I hear you, Son."

On one early morning run, just as I finished a line of a prayer, a massive owl with its wings spread wide swooshed out of the pitch-black sky directly in front of me! Frankly, it was quite terrifying at first. This thing was huge and so beautiful! I was immediately blown away and confident that God had just acknowledged my prayer! Isn't God so good? My favorite bird sign from God happened not too long ago. I was driving along the coast of Pensacola Bay with my sunroof open. I was praying for guidance, assistance, knowledge, and provision to help me with a certain situation. As I prayed, the most beautiful bald eagle flew right above my car just ahead of me. And, yes, we have bald eagles here. Enter mind-exploding! Writing it in words just doesn't come close to the experience. This majestic, awesome bird soared above my sunroof nearly my entire ride home. And guess what? That prayer was answered on all fronts … just like that. BOOM! Folks, this stuff just doesn't happen to everyone. We must be "tapped in" as I call it. We must be aware of our surroundings and what God is saying to us. He uses His beautiful creations to let us know "Hey, kid. I'm right here. In fact, I've always been here and will never leave."

Ask the LORD your God for a sign, whether in the deepest depths or in the highest heights. (Isaiah 7:11).

What does being a joy-full entrepreneur mean to you, and how is this emphasized in your daily life?

Being a joy-full entrepreneur means total freedom to me. I'm free to make ethical and logical decisions for my life and business. I never had that type of freedom working a W2 job, not even close. There were many practices that I abhorred, but what could I do or say? Well, I said plenty, believe you me, and often to my own detriment. And at that point, I could do or say no more. So there I was working in an environment that didn't fit my personal views and faith postures. And because doing the right thing is so important to me and vital to my ministry and business, I had to make some hard decisions and take a leap of faith.

Making that leap of faith has made me a free man, and it's oh so Joy-Full! It allows me to do the right thing every day, which is so vital to my ministry and business. I also don't miss out on the special moments with my family that I used to miss working for someone else. I take my daughters to and from school, and I have way more time with them during the day than ever before. It's just been a win-win for me.

I'm also free to drop most things at a moment's notice to serve someone in need. It's extremely fulfilling to be able to say, "Yes!" to things that I couldn't have done prior to starting this entrepreneurial journey.

And the best part ... I am able to go into my office, shut the door, and spend time with Him, exactly like I'm doing right now. By the way, I prayed for Him to write this for me. Take that ChatGPT! When one has God, who needs AI? Well, we do use it from time to time, but you get my point. I would normally drop a smiley emoji here. Know that I'm smiling right now.

So if the Son sets you free, you will be free indeed (John 8:38).

What wisdom or encouragement would you give someone who has never blended their faith and business strategy as one? How has it aided in your profitability?

To say that I have struggled in my business life is an understatement! Oftentimes, I'd try to do everything myself. I had a hard time delegating and handing off tasks because of my "lead-singer" ego. I often felt smarter, more energetic, and more focused on the task at hand than others that I was supposedly working "with." WRONG! I'm certain that this won't be a shock to you, dear reader, but that way of thinking and doing *never* works out. Never!

When I took the leap of faith, all I had was God. I didn't have a plan, finances, physical partners, nothing—but I did have Him! I hit my knees every morning nearly begging God to be a lamp to my feet and light my path! I prayed for Him to teach me how to be more faithful. That's a big one right there. Ask God to teach you! He will! As I shared in *The Joy-Full Entrepreneur* (Volume 1), I had to give it ALL up to God. "Here, Lord, I give you me, my health, my wife, my children, my BUSINESS. I have let go of the reins. I am no longer in control of my future. Father, I give it all to you." That prayer right there changed everything in my life and business! Suddenly, people who needed my help seemed to just appear out of nowhere ... people who weren't friends of mine on social media, people who didn't know about my band (I perform concerts for thousands), people who had never seen my TV show. I didn't know these people, y'all! What felt like miracles were exactly that! There's no other explanation. God brought these deals to me on a golden platter. Served 'em right up to me! "Here you go, good and faithful servant." I flipped the house across the street, the house next door, the house diagonally across the street! Folks, that stuff doesn't just happen ... but, oh, yes it does! For those of us who believe and are faithful to Him, anything is possible! As I've previously stated, there is nothing like the power of prayer! Pray for it all! Pray for God to show you who to serve in your business. Make that prayer daily and watch what happens. I 100 percent guarantee you that your mind will be blown and that your business will be more successful than ever!

To put this into perspective, in the nearly fifteen years at my former W2, I only received one raise, maybe two. I made the exact same amount of income each year as I watched the department's profit grow. Ready for the good part? Last year was my first full year running my real estate investment business, and I nearly tripled my income! Don't *you* want that for you and your family? Can you imagine earning three times what you earn right now simply because you gave your business to God? Yes! Then all you need to do, and it's so simple (not easy but simple), is to go to God in prayer right now, and let Him know that you're giving Him the reins to your business. It will be one of the best decisions that you ever made.

Hey! Guess What? I Love You!

*Commit your works to
the Lord [submit and trust
them to Him], And your plans
will succeed [if you respond to
His will and guidance]*

Proverbs 16:3, AMP.

Sharayah Gonzales

My name is Sharayah Diane Gonzales. I am an entrepreneur; business owner; and founder of SDG Solutions LLC offering accounting, bookkeeping, tax preparation, and business consulting as well as the executive director of the Medina Senior Center/Meals on Wheels Medina County. I love helping, connecting with and serving others, and learning new things. I also love and enjoy the arts of all forms, including movies, music, dance, singing, acting (especially musical theater), or any art that moves my heart and tells a meaningful and transformational story with a powerful message.

Chapter 7
Start Connecting the Dots ...

Would you describe your entrepreneurial adventure as a solution, a sign, or a wonder based on your personal testimony and experience? Explain.

My entrepreneurial adventure has definitely been and continues to be a wonder—going from being jobless to Executive Director of our county's Meals on Wheels nonprofit organization in less than a year is inexplicable. I could not have imagined being in the position I am in currently. A little over two years ago, I would have told you that I enjoyed where I worked. The people I worked with were like family, and I had a seemingly flexible schedule and understanding bosses who allowed me the time to pursue one of my dreams of performing. I was learning to enjoy and embrace my career path and was beginning to see how what I did made a difference in our clients' lives and in the lives of my coworkers. I could even see myself retiring at that firm. All the dots seemed to be starting to connect ...

> *No eye has seen, no ear has heard, and no mind has imagined what God has prepared for those who love him (1 Corinthians 2:9, NLT).*

As mentioned before, I enjoyed my job, my career, and the people I worked with, including the relationship I developed with my bosses. As business owners and quasi-parents, I considered both he and his wife mentors. So you can imagine the shock and disappointment I felt when he made unwanted sexual advances. The heartbreaking realization that my whole life would change was devastating. Not only was my trust broken, but his actions would ultimately hurt his wife who was my friend and someone I cared about deeply. It seemed so unfair that the actions of one individual could affect so many people and destroy so much of my life. I lost my friend and mentor (his wife), personal and professional relationships, my career, income source, retirement 401(k), health insurance, and the work family I loved. The loss of all this, especially the loss of his wife's friendship (she chose not to believe me), was painful.

Despite the piercing pain of the loss I immediately felt and knew I would continue to feel, I had a peace—His peace—knowing my only option and God's will was to quit my job. Somehow God had better plans for me. My workplace was no longer a comfortable or safe environment, and staying would have sent the message that my boss's actions weren't *that* bad and were even acceptable. It was as if God finally said, "Instead of working hard to the point of exhaustion and putting in the tireless effort for someone else's company, it is time for you to spread your wings and fly, to pursue the dreams and goals I have placed in you. You have worked so hard at serving others, now the time has come to finally fight for yourself." At the time, it was hard for me to imagine specifically what God had planned and prepared for me.

Over the course of about eight months, God would send the individuals and mentors I needed to help me heal, provide job opportunities and experiences, and develop the entrepreneurial skills that God had been teaching me over the last several years. One of these mentors, of course, was Tamra Andress who by her example, her heart for God and others, her joy, and her vulnerability helped open my eyes to the plan God had for me all along.

Now to Him who is able to do immeasurably more than all we ask or imagine, according to His power that is at work within us, to Him be glory in the church and in Christ Jesus throughout all generations, for ever and ever! Amen. (Ephesians 3:20-21).

What Christ-like solutions have you discovered that make your day-to-day business manageable and fruitful?

I am nowhere near perfect, but I've noticed that when I begin my day with prayer, meditation, and conversation with the Lord—rather than immediately diving into tasks—I experience a greater sense of His peace throughout the day. This becomes especially evident when facing challenging situations or engaging in difficult conversations.

> *The way to start something new is to quit something else. —Bob Goff*

Embracing simplicity has also proven helpful in making day-to-day business manageable and fruitful. I strive for simplicity, not just in the three main tasks needing to be accomplished that day but, more importantly, keeping in mind the two greatest commandments: to love God and to love others. By prioritizing relationships over tasks, and practicing empathy, understanding, and grace, I find that my interactions become more meaningful and fulfilling.

> *I've learned that people will forget what you said, people will forget what you did, but people will never forget how you made them feel. —Most credited to Maya Angelou*

I've also learned the importance of staying focused on the present moment, showing love and kindness to the person in front of me, and attending to the immediate tasks at hand. Instead of becoming overwhelmed by the entire To-Do list for the week or month, I concentrate on what's right in front of me today. This approach helps reduce stress and allows me to engage more effectively with each task.

What signs have been given to you along the way that have led you to say yes to exploring and activating your entrepreneurial spirit?

Going back to the Old Testament verse that 1 Corinthians 2:9 is based on, Isaiah 64:4 (NLT) says, *For since the world began, no ear has heard and no eye has seen a God like you, who works for those who wait for him!*

It definitely seemed like a long waiting period and multiple signs (some I completely missed or ignored) to get to where God needed me to be. It also involved the daily renewing of my mind, healing from the pain and rejection, consulting with loved ones and mentors, following my God-given talents, and, ultimately, dependence on Him.

My first job right out of college was as a staff auditor in public accounting. I did well as a part-time intern but was not prepared for the real working world after graduation. I did not expect the number of hours involved (over sixty-hour work weeks) and did not realize how "green" I was and how little I knew. For someone who was salutatorian of her class, graduated with both her bachelor's and master's degrees in four years, and had her self-worth wrapped up in accomplishments; my world came crashing down when I was let go from my first job. Looking back, I realize that my views on failure, perfectionism, and people-pleasing took me down into an unhealthy cycle for the next several years as I threw myself into my work trying to prove my worth.

I took another shot at auditing for a different public accounting firm, yet there was still a sense deep down in my spirit—a sign—that made me think there had to be more to life than this. I know now that there are times to persevere through failure and other times where it may be an indicator of not being where one is meant to be … discerning the difference is wisdom.

During the approximately seven years I spent in public accounting, my life mainly consisted of work, study for the CPA exam, eat, sleep, and repeat. In addition, the multiple close attempts at passing some of the four CPA exams were draining, time-consuming (120+ hours of study each section, each time), and discouraging. Although I passed one and was getting close to passing the other sections, I began to see this venture as a waste of time and money. On top of all of this, a limited social life and not eating well (due to a limited budget) added to my stress and caused my health to decline. The burnout was so extreme that my body was physically worn down, and I found myself unable to sit up for even an hour.

This situation was made even worse with the heartbreak of my grandparents unexpectedly passing away within a month of each other and my resulting feelings of regret along with the realization that I had taken for granted the time I had with my loved ones. Then the COVID pandemic shutdown happened…. It was once again a time of reflection and realization of how fragile life is. It was a beautiful representation, at least in our small town, of how a community could pull together to help one another when resources (from toilet paper to food) were scarce. Looking back, all these incidents could have been signs that I ignored … signs that God was trying to get my attention.

A couple of months into the COVID-19 shutdown, I was given the opportunity to take virtual private lessons and virtual musical theater classes. My instructors, Ginna Claire "GC" Mason and Mary Kate "MK" Morrissey, are two of my favorite Broadway performers. They supported and encouraged me and helped build my confidence in my acting and singing talents by urging all of their students to take risks on stage and in life. During one of my private lessons, MK also encouraged me not to dim my light for anyone out of fear of how they would react or what they might think of me or my art. That short season of my life was one of the most liberating and happiest I had experienced in a long while—and a possible indicator or "sign" that I was on the right track on my journey of growth.

It was during this time, however, that I was experiencing the unwanted sexual advances from my boss. I did not know what to do and hesitated to leave the place I had called home for so long. I explored every possible scenario in an attempt to find a way to stay, a way to cause the least amount of hurt to all involved. Although this difficult situation was a clear sign that I needed to leave my job, God sent me the largest sign (literally and physically) after I prayed for direction—a billboard right outside our office building that read, "THINK GOD." It felt as if I was on the edge of a cliff, leaving me no choice but to take a leap of faith. With two actions remaining in front of me—to share the truth with my boss's wife and to quit—I knew that I had to trust that God had equipped me to soar or that He would catch me if I fell.

Another significant turning point occurred on February 17, 2021, when I joined the Clubhouse app. The "Breakfast with Champions" room became a source of motivation, education, and inspiration from diverse speakers, such as Glenn Lundy, Christin Kingsbury, Marcus Black, Danelle Delgado, and Tamra Andress. In a short amount of time, I felt like I was learning at hyper speed. These conversations eventually led me to attend my first in-person Kingdom Entrepreneur business conferences. At the 100X Expansion conference in California and the Grow your Business for God's Sake conference in Kentucky, I finally met some of the most amazing like-minded and like-hearted entrepreneurs who helped guide the way for me during a very difficult season. After months of heartbreak, I finally felt I was on the right track and at home. And although there were times of difficulty where I felt what the Israelites must have been feeling in the desert—lost and wanting to return to the familiar but harmful circumstances in my own personal "Egypt," I reminded myself that growth and transformation take time and perseverance. Amazingly enough, only God could have orchestrated that exactly one year later on February 17, 2022, my LLC was formed!

As I reflect on this journey, I see the divine hand of God carefully planting seeds of growth and learning throughout every experience. Just like the stories of Joseph and other biblical figures, I am reminded that

God can turn what may have seemed like negative or challenging situations into opportunities for good and growth.

The foundation of my growth was laid during college with the National Society of Leadership and Success teaching me valuable lessons on masterminding and accountability. Additionally, various professors and teachers acted as guiding lights, shaping my path in profound ways.

After college, I encountered my fair share of failures, but I now realize that these were vital growth opportunities that built my perseverance and character. I learned that failure is not something to fear; rather, it serves as a catalyst for faster learning than perfection ever could. Embracing a higher perspective, I understood that a continuous renewal of the mind is essential, as stated in Romans 12:2.

During daily commutes to work, sometimes a two-hour round trip, I turned to audiobooks on entrepreneurship, self-help, and personal development. These moments of learning became invaluable as I ventured into the realm of entrepreneurship.

Moreover, the skills acquired from my previous jobs and the public accounting firms are still relevant in my current pursuits. Regardless of my future decision to test for the CPA again, the years spent studying for it have instilled in me not only a deeper understanding of my job but also the virtues of discipline and perseverance.

> *Change is inevitable. Growth is optional.*
> *—John C Maxwell*

Looking back, I find comfort in knowing that no experience is wasted in the hands of God. Each challenge, setback, and learning opportunity has contributed to shaping me into the person I am today—a person driven by a higher purpose and guided by the lessons of the past. It is in these moments of reflection that we start connecting the dots and realize how much we've grown. With gratitude in my heart, I embrace the journey ahead, trusting that God's hand will continue to transform what was once meant for evil into something good in my life.

Who biblically has been a consistent mentor in your pursuit of excellence as an entrepreneur? What are their unique character traits and how have they modeled being a joy-full entrepreneur well?

Joseph in the Old Testament has been an inspiring mentor in my pursuit of excellence as an entrepreneur. His admirable traits, including integrity, resilience, wisdom, patience, forgiveness, leadership, humility, perseverance, faith, and a servant's heart have left a profound impact on me. Joseph's unwavering integrity was evident in his faithful devotion to God and his refusal to yield to temptation from Potiphar's wife. He exemplified the importance of doing what is right and speaking the truth, even when faced with false accusations and being thrown in prison. Joseph's resilience in navigating setbacks and his profound belief and trust that God knows the truth and will bring about restoration in due time is a testament to his unwavering faith.

Throughout his thirteen-year journey from the pit to the prison to the palace, Joseph embraced each season of life with patience, trust, and perseverance. His servant's heart led him to selflessly help those around him, finding opportunities to make a positive impact wherever he was. Joseph performed everything with excellence, understanding that he was ultimately serving the Lord as Colossians 3:23 states. Moreover, his ability to forgive his brothers after their betrayal and wrongdoing serves as a powerful lesson in compassion and reconciliation. Joseph's story continues to inspire me to pursue excellence, embrace challenges with resilience, and nurture an integrous servant's heart in all that I do.

What has been your biggest challenge or trial in keeping your joy as an entrepreneur and leader?

I would have to say my biggest challenge in keeping my joy is being intentional in making time for much needed rest, relationships, and recreation. Rest is often overlooked, as I tend to get caught up in the never-ending to-do list, especially when I forget to start my day with Him and from a place of peace. I experienced extreme burnout in my public accounting years, but I've come to the realization that the cause of these stress-related issues was rooted in me feeling that I was not doing enough and the fact that I was seeking the approval of others because of those who had rejected me. The only One that I needed approval from was God.

As an introvert, it is my natural tendency to want to stay at home, rationalizing that I need to finish work. I allowed business to create a distance between me and others, leaving me feeling accomplished but lonely. And over the years, a few tough relationships (romantic and friendships) caused deep hurts, betrayal, and rejection. Some resulted in me having to make the tough decisions to let go of unhealthy and/or one-sided relationships to make room for the new and the freedom to be myself. These experiences have caused me difficulty in trusting and cultivating new friendships; therefore, I have now made it a point to be prayerful, to allow discernment to guide the relationships to pursue, and to trust God to surround me with the individuals He ordained. I have come to realize that I deeply value quality time with the people I care about and have resolved to guard and nurture the relationships that nourish my spirit.

The word *recreation*, broken down as *re-creation*, holds the key to bringing renewal and refreshment. To combat the tendency to overlook recreation, I consciously make time for activities that bring joy and rejuvenation. This ensures that I'm not just focused on work but also making space for new and enriching experiences. Some of these experiences include attending conferences, such as FounderCon (formerly Grow For God); fellowshipping with others; attending theater productions or movies; traveling; and exploring new cities.

Writing some of this chapter in my great aunt and uncle's backyard—the tall Oregon trees blowing in the wind and the distant ocean waves crashing—makes me appreciate these quiet moments of rest. These quiet pauses make it easier to hear His voice and reflect on what is truly important: focusing on the moment and the people in front of us and realizing the need to schedule this more often—time for Him, family, and for others.

In summary, my pursuit of joy drives my intentionality to incorporate rest, to nurture meaningful relationships, and to engage in refreshing activities. By embracing these aspects, I am discovering a more fulfilling and balanced approach to life.

How has your faith been sharpened as an entrepreneur?

I was at a job for a little over four years, pretty much the same deadlines each year, and was finally starting to feel I had control. I statistically showed improvements year-over-year, increasing the amount of clients and projects I was able to work on. Dangerously, the comfort and stability of my job allowed me to fall into the pride of self-reliance, which made me believe that I was the main reason for my success. I never want to make that mistake again. Thankfully, the constant state of change as an entrepreneur has been the biggest force behind the sharpening of my faith. The unknown pushes me to rely on Him in all that I do and to be grateful for the blessings I have now.

Currently, I have a good client base to whom I provide consulting, tax, bookkeeping, and payroll services. With hiring my first intern came feelings of excitement and the weight of responsibility, as it provides the opportunity for my company to grow and serve more clients in need while also offering my intern tools for a successful career and balanced life.

My current position as the executive director and financial administrator of our county's Meals on Wheels has been a blessing and a faith journey where I am able to finally put into practice what I've learned over the years (in theory and by observation) about leading a team, managing operations, and building relationships. It has also helped me to develop new skills, such as understanding grants, state funding, building projects, marketing, fundraising, and so much more. I'm also extremely grateful for this opportunity to use these gifts to serve our community and our seniors, one of the most vulnerable populations in our community.

Closing Thoughts

Embracing the path of entrepreneurship has been a journey of profound growth and self-discovery, unlocking opportunities that go far beyond personal and worldly success. With character built from perseverance through suffering and despite the inevitable hardships, this entrepreneurial pursuit has gifted me with a newfound sense of hope as the scriptures remind us in Romans 5:1–5. It has become my purpose, my calling, to help my family and others uncover and nurture their God-given potential. It fills my heart with immeasurable joy and fulfillment being a mentor to those around me, knowing that my experiences and insights not only can guide them on their journey to success but also inspire and uplift others.

This entrepreneurial venture has reinvigorated my faith, knowing I will succeed if I continue to refocus my efforts on aligning these plans with God's divine purpose for my life and for others. With the freedom and flexibility that entrepreneurship affords, I can now embrace the moments and experiences that truly matter, leaving a heartfelt legacy of love, inspiration, and growth for generations to come. The journey of entrepreneurship has opened doors to a world of possibilities, and I am grateful for the blessings it has brought into my life.

One of my favorite quotes that I apply to both life and business is "Do not go where the path may lead, go instead where there is no path and leave a trail,"

Ralph Waldo Emerson.

Laura Hicks

Laura is a wife, mother, and grandmother residing in Washington State with her husband. Sales has been in her blood from a very young age. She was hired into sales in her first corporate job at Acme Staple Company, and it has remained a lifelong passion. From there her career expanded into different technical fields, such as lasers, electro optics, polyurethane coated fabrics, and information technology. She has also been involved in real estate investing, writing and speaking, and has owned a retail jewelry store. She developed and grew several successful companies and enjoys helping others through training, coaching, and mentoring. She has also interviewed some of the top business authors in order to share their experience and wisdom with others. She loves figuring out how to enroll others in her vision, and her passion is to leave an impact and lead others to attain success through businesses, building legacy, financial independence, and creating impact by giving back through philanthropy. Things that give her joy and keep her growing are hiking, gardening, kayaking, baking, photography, reading, spending time with friends, and vacationing with family.

Chapter 8
Creating Your Unique Trail

Would you describe your entrepreneurial adventure as a solution, a sign, or a wonder based on your personal testimony and experience? Explain.

My entrepreneurial adventure is a bit of all of the above. I learned early on that I could enroll others into things that I was excited or passionate about, and this entrepreneurial journey has been a *solution* to my need to share what I have learned with others in order to help them on their journeys. In the world of business, there are so many things that are not taught, things like being a servant leader, owning your emotions, and understanding that money is a tool.

I also believe that my career path has been directed by many *signs*. These undeniable road signs have occurred throughout my life and keep repeating in my ambitions and goals. Although I had no idea that I would pursue a career in sales, the pattern was set very early in my life with my first official sales pursuit—selling Girl Scout cookies. I also remember when I was in third grade and figured out how to make bracelets and sell them in school. In turn, I would share what I had done and teach others how to do the same. My love of sales and training others had begun!

Wonder has also been an important part of my entrepreneurial journey. I have always had an innate curiosity and a drive to challenge myself to grow. Wonder to me is a wide-eyed approach to the world that is inspired by others and fueled by my desire to reach the places that others have already achieved. Wonder also manifests through creativity. I learned early on that I could use my creativity to make something and trade it for money. My creations included such things as pot holders (on my loom kit), macramé plant hangers, flavored toothpicks, and baked goods. Over and over these sales opportunities presented themselves as did a very clear entrepreneurial path to trade a skill for money. Looking back, I would say that my entrepreneurial experience has been guided by solutions, wonders, and signs—signs that are now so obvious to me, as with most things in hindsight.

How is "wonder" a part of your rhythm as a leader, visionary, and business builder?

I'm constantly inspired to grow through catching the lessons and the gained experience of others. I was fascinated in my early career to get better at sales. A big inspiration and foundational piece for me were the teachings of Zig Ziglar, an author, salesman, and motivational speaker. Every day I would listen to his lessons and be influenced by who he was and how he lived. He was an example of someone who was joyful. Zig's examples of how to work with and treat others set the foundation for my sales career. He talked about focusing on *helping* over *selling* and encouraged solving problems by uncovering their pain points. I always tell people that great sales start with providing a match to a need. And over the years, I have shared Zig's wisdom with as many people as I could.

> *You can have everything in life you want, if you will*
> *just help enough other people get what they want.*
> *—Zig Ziglar*

The true wonder in being an entrepreneur is the impact that can be had as a leader through the sharing of wisdom that is acquired through experience. I remember hearing, when I was younger, that knowledge is power. I now know that is not true. There is nothing wrong with a quest for knowledge and information, but it really becomes valuable when you utilize it. I now share with people that *applied* knowledge is power.

Through my career as a Senior Sales Director with Mary Kay, leading ninety sales consultants, I was exposed to John C. Maxwell, a well-known faith-based leader, writer, and mentor. I was able to meet him in person and go through study classes he provided. I have read most of his books (he has written a substantial quantity) and a good part of his writings focusing on leadership. John models what he writes about in his life and applies the knowledge that he has acquired. His phenomenal success speaks to how many lives he has impacted through his work helping others. I love this quote of his on leadership and vision: "Good leaders must communicate vision clearly, creatively, and continually. However, the vision doesn't come alive until the leader models it." It is so important as a leader to explain the vision of where you want to take your business and then to share that vision with others and how they can contribute to it so that they become a part of it and get excited about the journey. This doesn't mean that you have every answer, but you must have confidence in your ability to get there, all the while modeling that it is acceptable to make mistakes and course corrections as you move forward. Part of this journey is the wonder of exactly how your plan and vision will evolve and grow as your business succeeds.

Another one of his quotes that I love is: "The greatest mistake we make is living in constant fear that we will make one." To me, *wonder* is a part of creativity, and if you are living in fear of making mistakes, then you are not risking, experimenting, failing, learning, and growing. It reminds me of being suspended in space and time, not making decisions. It is hard to build forward momentum or traction when you are not moving to begin with. Personally, I have had to grow through the fear and have tackled that part of me that doesn't want to make mistakes. It is human to be messy.

That, too, is part of the wonder of being human and a business builder. Through failures and mistakes, you can reflect on and distill what really works. Fear of making mistakes comes in part from the belief that others are watching and judging. You must feel free to walk in your own shoes, choose your own path, and embrace the lifting experience of gained wisdom that you have gathered through your collective experiences.

What does being a joy-full entrepreneur mean to you and how is this emphasized in your daily life?

As I contemplated this question, I looked up the definition of joy from a number of different sources. They all included such sentiments as a sense of well-being, great appreciation or pleasure, happiness from success, delight, and elation. Every day, both with and through other entrepreneurs, I get to experience their struggles, dreams, and successes and help them get to the next steps along their journey. It is my privilege to be part of this process in the lives of the individuals who cross my path. This is a joy-full experience for me, helping others in any way that I can. Because I love what I do, I show up joy-full for the people that I am connected with.

This question also brought to mind some practical wisdom in the area of being joy-full. I learned long ago that owning our emotions is a key piece to getting where we want to be in this life. So in order to progress towards my goals, I began to focus on and develop my emotional intelligence. Take the time to reflect on how your emotions impact your entrepreneurial journey. Do you see yourself as a perpetual victim? Do you find yourself thinking: "My boss is always taking the credit." "My family is always criticizing me." "_____ made me cry." Being an entrepreneur is not necessarily easy, and our emotions can sometimes take a beating. When this happens, these feelings can impact our life, our business, and our joy. Learning to develop my emotional intelligence was one of the most useful skills I have acquired as an adult, and it allows me to live an intentionally joy-full life.

What has been your biggest challenge or trial in keeping your joy as an entrepreneur and leader?

I have always been an optimist and attribute that to the people I spent time with growing up. My grandma Ruth was a family friend. She was strong, independent, creative, and inquisitive, with a spirit of sharing information she had learned with others. My grandma Muriel was the same, with interests in gardening and practical things, like where to find asparagus in the spring and why it was important to open a passbook savings account. Both of these amazing women no longer had men in their lives and were great examples of how to overcome adversity and live productive and inspirational lives. I'm sure life was not always easy, but they approached each day as a new opportunity.

These early lessons taught me that I can control my state of being despite the circumstances around me. That was eye-opening for me, even as a natural optimist. If I wake up on a rare morning and I'm grumpy, I am able to acknowledge it in order to understand why I have chosen that state of mind. And because I not only control it but own it, I can ask, "What can I do to change it?" The first step is to decide that I want a different emotional state. Next, I have to decide on how to get there. Is that taking a walk, having my favorite cup of tea, calling someone who always makes me laugh, or simply sitting quietly with myself and choosing another state of being altogether.

This skill helps me on my entrepreneurial journey because not every day is necessarily an easy one. It seems like there are always new things to learn and problems waiting to be solved. It does make the doing easier, however, when you have an understanding that it all starts with how you are "being"—your emotional state. The easiest person to beat up is yourself. Diving into entrepreneurship is an experience that requires you to give yourself some grace, some forgiveness, and some positive input.

There is a deep vein of appreciation for my grandmothers who lived independently and freely gave many lessons in how to navigate life. They set the foundation in those early lessons on emotional management and knowing that, no matter what challenges are thrown my way, I can always choose how I will respond and overcome. Living in joy is much easier than being destructive and later attempting to make amends. A dear friend of mine shared an example of this principle through a story. When he was young and newly married, his wife baked him an apple pie. Upon tasting it, he noticed the apples were crunchy and offered to his new wife that his mother could teach her how to make apple pie. In their long, happy marriage, she never baked him another. He said he could never undo the damage or destruction from something that never needed to be said. We laughed over this story as we ate the apple pie (without crunchy apples) that I had made for them, but it stuck with me—you can't unsay things. While there is a need for great open communication, choose to share the good with others—choose to sow life into them with your words. Be joy and bring joy. You can have joy, experience joy, and share joy regardless of your bank account or self-defined level of success.

How do you market your business and faith? What is your belief system in showcasing one over the other and how have you come to peace with your personal solution?

I market my business and faith in a low-key way and choose to be a good example at all times for those around me (which is also leading by example). I believe in doing unto others as they wish—just a little different than the "golden rule." We are all different, but we all have the same basic desires to succeed, to be seen, to be in community, to leave evidence of our existence, and to be cared about by someone. In each of these areas, every person has an individual definition of what that looks like. Take community as an example. Some people want to know and interact with everyone, while some simply want to hang back and learn from others. Treating others as they wish means not imposing your will on them but discovering how they operate and meeting them where they are in order to help them bridge to where they want to be. It also includes never expecting others to do what you are unwilling to do yourself.

What wisdom or encouragement would you give someone who has never blended their faith and business strategy as one? How has it aided in your profitability?

I was told from a very young age that you can do anything you are willing to put the work into. Entrepreneurship is the same. I would add some additional wisdom: Find a way to work smarter and not harder. One way to do that is by putting systems in place that allow you to work "on" your business, not "in" your business. It was in the book, *The E Myth Revisited*, by Michael E. Gerber, where I learned that most entrepreneurs start businesses because they are good technicians at what they do. Gerber teaches that every business owner is comprised of three very different personalities: the Technician, the Manager, and the Entrepreneur. Each of these personalities approaches and deals with the business from a different perspective. The Technician is the doer. She loves her craft and is focused on doing the work. The Manager thrives on order, routines, planning, and systems. She is pragmatic and loves predictability. The Entrepreneur is the visionary, the dreamer. She is creative and sees where she wants the business to go.

One of these three personalities is probably your area of strength, while the other two will compete for your attention. In a perfect world, we would be able to balance these three roles with no difficulties; however, that is not usually the case. You can choose to have someone coach you through the process of growth as an entrepreneur, or you can go it alone. I have done both, but I have learned along the way that most people need to enlist help.

You also need to ask yourself what your goals are for the company. Knowing your goals can help you to decide if you want to be a solopreneur and go it alone. As a solopreneur you will probably sit in the Technician role while running and controlling everything. This, however, will limit your business to your personal bandwidth. You may instead choose to evaluate your key strengths, decide which role you would be best in, and then hire people who can fill in the missing pieces. There is not a right or wrong choice. Whether you choose to enlist the expertise of a coach or hire people to help you grow your business, remember, you do not have to take on entrepreneurship alone. Asking for help was one of my most challenging lessons along the way.

Once your business is up and running, there is an easy litmus test you can use to figure out if you really have a sustainable business. Ask yourself if you could leave it for a week or two or a month and it would still make money. That is one of the things we do at ScaleUp Biz. We teach owners how to grow and scale successfully by effectively improving your bottom-line without the growing pains. And as your business grows, have faith and trust that the right people, connections, tools, and resources will be put in your path as you continue on this amazing entrepreneurial journey. My understanding of this journey has grown through investing in myself. These investments have always created a multiplier effect through new information implemented and the relationships gained through community and connections.

I also took lessons from author and start-up advisor, Tim Ferriss, on different ways of thinking about life. In his book, *The 4-Hour Workweek*, he asks us to consider what we would do if we knew that we would not fail. That made me reflect on how big would I draw out my goals if failure were not a possibility. It made me realize I was keeping myself small and not using all of the talents that had been given to me (which would result in me making less of an impact during my time on this planet). It also made me do a reset on the way I thought and has enabled me to start not one business but several and find success through taking bigger risks than I might have otherwise. And it all comes full circle with one of his quotes that supports what I said earlier about knowledge and power: "Information is useless if not applied to something important or if you will forget it before you have a chance to apply it."

Closing Thoughts

Your path is unique, but you do not walk it alone whether you experience it through your faith, the universe and exchanged energy, or the humans you share interactions with while on this planet. You have unlimited potential to tap and a wealth of human resources through whom you can receive knowledge and wisdom for each phase of your journey and for every area of your life. Zig Ziglar, who I spoke of earlier, taught that the Wheel of Life contained seven areas or "spokes": Mental, Spiritual, Physical, Family, Financial, Personal, and Career. His question was "Which one of those seven areas did God create you not to be successful in?" No matter what your beliefs, it is a great question to ask. Why can't you have it all? It is not success in business to the exclusion of everything else. I know I'm not alone in thinking that lots of things are not important if I cannot share my success with others in my life.

At ScaleUp Biz, we love helping entrepreneurs focus on the one thing that will move their business to the next stage, phase, or milestone. There is a process and assessment we take our clients through so that they not only understand their business but their vision for impact. We can then define the steps, time frames, goals, project management, and resources needed. Taking one step at a time, we assist them in charting their course, unlocking the joy through less overwhelm, releasing more creativity through tangible progress, and unlocking the success they are seeking to achieve. You only have one life; let us help you make the most of it! You can find a bit more about what we do at scaleupbiz.com.

If you have raced with men on foot and they have worn you out, how can you compete with horses?

Proverbs 12:5.

Julianne Kirkland

Julianne Kirkland is a wife of one and a mom of six. As an international best-selling author, TEDx Speaker, AWAKE Conference and Next Level Faith founder, former Mastery Trainer for Tony Robbins, and an Integrated Identity life coach for high-achieving business professionals, Julianne uses her expertise as an Overcomer Strategist to help turn life's stumbling blocks into stepping stones. Through her signature ARISE Formula framework, Julianne has helped many around the world discover that creating a joyful life they love, doesn't have to be so hard!

Chapter 9
The Multiplier

Would you describe your entrepreneurial adventure as a solution, a sign, or a wonder based on your personal testimony and experience? Explain.

My entrepreneurial journey has included all three! As Ecclesiastes 4:12 (NLT) reminds us, "A triple braided cord is not easily broken." I have yet to experience a sign or wonder that did not inherently create a solution to a problem I was facing. And it's because you believe you have "the solution" to someone's problem that you even become an entrepreneur in the first place.

Once you begin to invite God into your business, all aspects of it, you see His work in everything that you do. The revelation of that work might not be apparent at the exact moment it is occurring, but I truly believe that each strand that makes up the tapestry of my entrepreneurial adventure has been woven together with solutions, signs, and wonders.

One of my favorite examples has to do with our children. My husband and I had two amazing little boys, two years apart, and we wanted to try for a little girl. And although this may seem to be solely a personal adventure, the truth is the solutions, signs, and wonders that were revealed to me through it would pierce the very heart of who I was becoming as an entrepreneur and impact every business decision I would make thereafter.

Much to our surprise, I ended up pregnant with twins. I just knew they would be twin girls, I mean how "picture perfect" would that family dynamic be? Two boys, two years apart, followed by twin girls? Yes, please!

This third pregnancy was smooth and easy going. There were no long days lying on the cool tile around my toilet like I had previously done with my two sons. No, this time was different; I couldn't help but feel highly favored and blessed … that was until I went in for a regularly scheduled sonogram and found out baby B no longer had a heartbeat.

I was desperate for answers that the doctor could not give. Speculation was not good enough; I wanted understanding. I wanted to know exactly what went wrong, and I wanted a guarantee that baby A would not encounter the same fate.

My doctor did the best she could to assure me baby A, being in a separate sac, should develop just fine. "Just fine?" Who wants "just fine" when it comes to the health and well-being of her child?

After several weeks of wrestling with God and the "why me" attitude, I finally began to relax and shift my attention to enjoying my growing belly and the baby that remained inside. That was until the following ultrasound appointment when baby A would follow in her sister's footsteps. The depression that ensued was an acute pain I had never felt before. My husband took the loss as a *sign* that we were not meant to have any more children.

How could that be? Did I not understand God after all? Wasn't He supposed to be a *good* father? This didn't feel good, nor did it feel very father-like. Even if I had the "correct" answer right in front of me, I wouldn't have been able to see it clearly through my haze of despair and burning tears.

I did the only thing I could muster the strength to do; from a broken heart I pleaded with God to not let this loss be the end of our story.

> *"As the heavens are higher than the earth, so are my ways higher than your ways and my thoughts than your thoughts"* (Isaiah 55:9).

Turns out, it wasn't the end of our story, and our loss would be fully redeemed in a way ONLY God could do—QUADRUPLETS! Yes, you read that right … God restored the twins we lost with quadruplets, and we were left in complete awe in the *wonder* of how God took our former sorrow and gave us "double for our trouble."

What signs have been given to you along the way that have led you to say yes to exploring and activating your entrepreneurial spirit?

Quadruplets were on the way, and they would be the very *sign* I needed to remind me how God can do super abundantly more than we dare ask or think or imagine (Ephesians 3:20). This would be a sign I would lean on repeatedly throughout my entrepreneurial journey.

And to be honest, this sign wasn't revealed to me just so I could utilize it in my "work." NO! You, me, we are all created in the image of God, and just how the human experience is woven into a beautiful tapestry, so is the manifold wisdom of God with all its many angles, hues, and dimensions of God's knowledge and application to *all* things.

You are not just what you do, and I don't believe God gives revelation that is only applicable to one area of your life, even though it might seem that way in some circumstances. His ways are higher! The inspiration from the revelation is meant to produce fruit in all areas where you are intentional about the activation of it!

The "sign" of multiplication through the embodiment of carrying and having quadruplets was not meant to just show me how God can take a loss of two and make it a gain of four. The sign was not OF multiplication after all; the sign *was* multiplication! And my babies were simply a physical representation of that. I was now, without a doubt, a multiplier, and that attribute would become the catalyst to my bold spirit as an entrepreneur.

How is "wonder" a part of your rhythm as a leader, visionary, and business builder?

I cannot hear the word *wonder* without attaching *awe* to it. To me wonder and awe are the manifold presence of God. It is like breathing; the inhale is the wonder; it is something you take in. The awe is the exhale; it's your response. And what's more rhythmic than breathing?

The truth is, as a woman, daughter, wife, parent, founder, leader, visionary, entrepreneur ... whatever title(s) I may be functioning under during a particular season, they are all a part of me.

We are created in God's image, and He is three-in-one, the Holy Trinity. It makes absolute sense that we, too, are multifaceted beings. When our brains and bodies are operating in full alignment, we breathe automatically, as it is a process conducted by our involuntary nervous system. However, if the medulla (the part of the brain that controls these symptoms) were to become injured, the act of breathing would become much more intentional and might even require outside medical devices to aid the process. And even without injury, we can often find ourselves unintentionally holding our breath when we are in a stressful or intense situation.

Just like breathing, experiencing *wonder* is a choice and so is our response. When we are fully aligned and operating properly, the encounter is automatic. Then there are times when we have experienced trauma or are simply overwhelmed by our conditions and circumstances, and therefore we must be more intentional about receiving the wonder and responding in awe.

Because the presence of God is right there with us in everything we do, the opportunity to consistently operate in *wonder* is with us as well.

What does being a joy-full entrepreneur mean to you and how is this emphasized in your daily life?

"The joy of the Lord is your strength" (Neh. 8:10). I have always been told how strong I am, especially when it comes to the whole "having quadruplets" thing. Even after my dad died, I was tasked with picking up his remains and giving a speech at his memorial because "I'm the strong one." And in general, I have always been tall, athletic, and physically strong. But for years I fought against embracing my strength, because to be honest, I never enjoyed the moments of life that called me to be strong. Yes, I love my kids, but at the same time, carrying, birthing, and potty training four of them at once was not what I would classify as an en**joy**able experience.

It was the same with losing my dad; I would have gladly surrendered the title of strong if it meant I got to have my dad back. If being strong meant going through more physical, mental, emotional, and spiritual pain … I was ready to throw in the towel.

That is until I wrote my first book, *Arise and Shine*. Going through the cathartic process of writing, editing, writing some more, and editing even more led me to the revelation that only through breakdown did I receive my breakthrough! My strength was never meant to be what carried me through; it was the loosening of my grip and the surrendering of my will that released His strength to cover it all. And in those moments where my strength was obvious and complemented by others, I was at my weakest. Those around me were seeing the joy of the Lord reflected through me—as strength!

Releasing the facade that "I had it all together" and embracing my weakness as an opportunity to let go and simply be in His presence was like being in the center of a tornado. No matter what circumstance was swirling around me, centered in Him was stillness, peace, joy … and that was my strength.

In my experience, to be anything but a joy-full entrepreneur would be incongruent. If you are an entrepreneur that seeks first His kingdom, seeks His face, and seeks to be surrendered to His will, then you can't help but embody the joy-full entrepreneur moniker—because it's no longer about what you do; it's about who you are, and even more so, it is about whose you are.

What has been your biggest challenge or trial in keeping your joy as an entrepreneur and leader?

Betrayal!

Betrayal is an inherent human experience and is used as a tool of the enemy to manifest destruction in every human life. As bold as that statement is, I can look back through my life, through scripture, and through any action/adventure movie and see betrayal in its many forms.

If betrayal is inevitable, why does it hurt so badly? The simple answer is that betrayal doesn't come from whom you'd expect. The attack of deception doesn't come from those who are openly against or indifferent to you. That kind is obvious and easier to deflect. No, the intense depth of pain caused by betrayal comes from your friends, your family, your inner circle, and those whom you have confided in, loved, and trusted.

Although I have experienced many betrayals throughout my life, the one that left me questioning my leadership ability and even my purpose was when I had several employees stage a coup within my salon company.

When I opened my salon company, I vowed to be the kind of boss that truly valued her people and was intentional about adding value to her people. I believed in investing in my people through the lens of their potential, not through their current conditions, circumstances, or behaviors.

I invested my time, energy, knowledge, and money—oh, so much money—all in a well-meaning effort to offer them a helping hand, when no one else would, and to be the voice of faith, when all they ever heard was doubt. I wasn't trying to make life easy … but perhaps hopeful. Hard work and perseverance were rewarded, and accountability was a set standard. I thought I had clearly checked off all the boxes for leadership success. But it turns out, as a business owner, the foundation for the growth of your company and all who walk through your doors cannot be built on potential, hopes, and dreams. Harsh? Perhaps, but it is an important lesson that every entrepreneur must learn, especially those who are kingdom-focused and truly want to serve people at the highest level.

So in spite of my good intentions, several of the women I had invested so highly in ultimately decided to lie and manipulate their way out of my company, and although that betrayal hurt, the one that pierced deeper still was the betrayal of myself. I had compromised my integrity, reasoned away the nudges of the Holy Spirit, and disregarded what I knew to be true—all in an attempt to appease my rebellious employees and be seen as the "good guy," the boss that "really does care."

I did care, but if I truly valued their growth like I claimed to do, I would have fired them a lot sooner. Not firing them became more about me than it was about them; I suppose I wanted to be their savior, the triumphant leader paving their path to Christ.

Even as I type these words, I feel my joy beginning to drain. It was my lack of true wisdom and my own ignorance about the importance of stewarding my "flock," instead of trying to save them, that resulted in both betrayals. The first was the betrayal of myself by compromising who God was calling me to be in order to fulfill what I thought the world was telling me I "should" be. And the second was the betrayal by the women under my care.

Betrayal of self is perhaps the most bitter pill to swallow. It creates within you a distrust that grows every time you think, "I don't know if I can do this?" "Will anyone actually care?" "Who am I to …?" These questions create an ideal environment for the enemy to distract, derail, and delay you from doing the very thing God has called you to.

So when you encounter betrayal, remember that your betrayal has a purpose. It is meant to be a *part* of your story, not the *whole* story. Let's be clear … Story? Yes! Stronghold? No!

You are not alone in your suffering, even though that is exactly what the enemy wants you to think. Don't give him the satisfaction of decreasing your joy; for the **joy** of the Lord is our strength!

What wisdom or encouragement would you give someone who has never blended their faith and business strategy as one? How has it aided in your profitability?

Living fragmented will never produce the abundant life that Jesus came to give you. We are not meant to suffer through life on Earth just to enjoy the abundance of heaven when we get there!

We are meant to live whole, complete, congruent lives "in the land of the living" (Psalm 27:13, NLT). Who you are and how you show up in this world can be fully aligned and expressed. If you are a woman of faith, the actions that embody that statement are not just manifested on Sunday morning!

One of the greatest lessons I learned after having quadruplets, losing my dad to Alzheimer's, and experiencing a gut wrenching betrayal (all within a few years) was that when I ignore parts of who I am in order to "fit in" with the world's expectations of who I "should" be, it's as if I am telling God, "I trust you ... just not with this."

You see, you are unique, not simply in your DNA profile, but in the way that you and only you can glorify God and in the way that He has called you to. Although others may have a similar call on their lives, there is a glory reserved specifically for you to give that delights the Father.

It makes me think of Christmas morning, watching all my kids unwrap their presents that we carefully curated for their enjoyment and well-being. Their reaction to the gifts is beautiful, but the joy that comes from seeing them use their gift day after day, especially if they are able to bless others through it ... yeah, that's what the gift was all about!

You have a gift; my guess would be that you have many. And sanctioning your gifts to only be applied in certain areas of your life is doing yourself, others, and God a disservice.

Showing up any other way than the fully integrated, most authentic version of you will always keep you from accessing the abundance of heaven's storehouse that was opened to you the moment you believed.

So if you are an entrepreneur concerned with how integrating your faith into your business strategy will affect your bottom line, I would invite you to shift your perspective. Creating business strategy without integrating your faith impedes the flow of abundance to *all* areas of your life.

Closing Thoughts

Dear reader, perhaps you picked up this book because you were seeking inspiration, motivation, or maybe a few practical tips and tricks to give you an advantage in your entrepreneurial journey. My hope is you have found all of these things plus many more. You see, because you have picked up this book, I know one thing for certain … your future is bright, all of it, not just your future in business. It is my hope that as you read through my chapter, you began to see your journey through my story, even though you may never have had quadruplets (but if you have, look a sister up, and we will have some great conversations). Everything you have ever been through God can and will use for *good*; that's His part; that's His promise. Your part in all of this is to continue to show up as all He created you to be, at all times, and everywhere you go.

For my verse, I chose from the book of Jeremiah. It says, "If you have run with men on foot and they have worn you out, how can you compete with horses" (Jeremiah 12:5). This verse has given me strength—when the typical, logical, and natural ways of this world seem to represent one stumbling block after another on my path as a kingdom entrepreneur. Those of us who have answered yes to this call of courage, however, have also said yes to "running with horses." We have said yes to living with purpose. We have said yes to shifting our perspective from seeing the stumbling block before us to asking how can this stepping stone be *for* us. The call on your life is great, and I'm cheering you on!

Trust in the Lord with all your heart and lean not on your own understanding; in all your ways submit to Him, and He will make your paths straight

Proverbs 3:5–6.

Dr. Michelle Marie Lappin

Dr. Michelle Marie Lappin is a Certified Wealth Coach who developed a passion for helping financially frustrated individuals realize that abundance is at their fingertips after climbing out of her own financial pit. As a mom and an Army Veteran, she understands what it's like to live paycheck-to-paycheck and be stuck under a mountain of debt. Growing up in the inner city and being raised by a single mother, Dr. Michelle Marie Lappin has gone from being a high-school dropout to completing a Doctorate of Business Administration through Capella University. She also works a full-time job outside of her coaching business and is an Adjunct Professor at Southern Nazarene University while spending her spare time with family and friends. Most importantly, Dr. Michelle Marie Lappin stands on her faith in Christ as the foundation of daily strength, guidance, and provision.

Chapter 10
Faith and Fulfillment Unleashed

Would you describe your entrepreneurial adventure as a solution, a sign, or a wonder based on your personal testimony and experience? Explain.

Describing my entrepreneurial journey as a wonder, truly captures its essence. According to the Merriam-Webster dictionary, *wonder* can be both a noun and an adjective. As a noun, it means something that causes astonishment and admiration. And as an adjective, it represents being super effective and efficient, beyond anything known or anticipated.

When I think of this entrepreneurial wonder as a noun, my mind gets flooded with thoughts. This adventure has taken me through ups and downs, leaving me breathless with astonishment and admiration. The challenges I faced were mind-blowing, but what really blew me away were the incredible responses from my followers and clients. I couldn't believe how many people reached out for my help. It left me in awe, and I'm still amazed to this day. That's where the admiration kicks in. It's incredible how the Lord uses me every single day to help others grow financially.

Now let's switch gears to the adjective form of *wonder*. Hold on tight because this is mind-boggling! Did you recall the adjective definition I shared earlier—"beyond anything known or anticipated?" It's like, whoa! That statement perfectly sums up this entrepreneurial adventure, don't you think? It reminds me of Psalm 139:14, where it says, "I praise you because I am fearfully and wonderfully made; your works are wonderful, I know that full well." God created me, witnessed every step of my journey, and carefully designed my whole life, including this amazing entrepreneurial adventure. It's no wonder it's been so effective and efficient, far surpassing anything I could have imagined.

As I wrap up my thoughts, one thing rings loud and clear: "Oh, what a wonder it has been!" It truly has been an incredible journey full of astonishment, admiration, and blessings beyond measure.

What Christ-like solutions have you discovered that make your day-to-day business manageable and fruitful?

First and foremost, let's talk about prayer. It's a crucial part of my daily life, especially when it comes to my business. Whenever I pray for divine appointments or ask God to guide me, amazing things happen!

Let me share a cool story. About two years ago, I had this awesome client, who was super successful. But then life threw her a curveball, and she lost her job. It was a tough time for her, but guess what? She's back working with me now, and we're going even deeper than before! I've learned so much about running my business effectively, and it's making a real difference for me and my clients.

And you know what else is super important? Being organized. I can hear you saying, "What does organization have to do with being Christ-like?" Well, let me drop some knowledge from 1 Corinthians 14:40 (NASB) on you: "But all things must be done properly and in an orderly manner." Boom! That's why organization matters.

Now picture this: I'm juggling a full-time job, running a multi-element business, teaching as an adjunct professor, and serving in ministry. Oh, and I'm trying to have a life too! Can you say hectic? That's why being organized is a lifesaver for me. Without it I'd be a hot mess, no doubt.

Everyone's way of staying organized is different, but I make a daily task list with my top priorities, along with a few extras if I have time. I categorize the tasks based on how long they'll take or if they have a specific deadline/appointment. It keeps me on track and in control.

And guess what? We're looping back to prayer, my friend! I don't just make a list and leave it at that. Nope, I take a moment to pray over it, asking God to guide me, give me the motivation I need, and provide the wisdom and resources to get things done according to His plan.

When I combine prayer and organization, miracles happen! I not only check off my daily tasks, but I do it with a sense of peace, knowing I'm aligned with God's will. And do you know what's even better? When we're in His will, unexpected blessings come our way (Galatians 6:9). Can I get a "heck yeah" for our amazing God?

What signs have been given to you along the way that have led you to say yes to exploring and activating your entrepreneurial spirit?

Let me tell you about the incredible journey that led me to explore and activate my entrepreneurial spirit. It all started during a time when I had just crawled out of my own financial pit. Friends and family, inspired by my own transformation, began approaching me for help with restructuring their budgets and paying off debt. Their trust in me and their belief in what I had accomplished was a pivotal moment for me. It was the moment that sparked the idea of starting a coaching business.

But you know what? I had never even considered becoming a financial coach before that moment. It was a whole new world opening up before me, and I couldn't help but say yes to exploring it. Little did I know, another amazing friend of mine was starting her own business as a business coach … go figure! She invited me to a small group meeting where she shared her vision, her mission, and her passion. And it ignited a fire within me! That beautiful friend, Tamra Andress (a.k.a. the woman behind the name on the cover of this book), became an integral part of my journey. We've not only worked together to build and scale my business, but this is our second Anthology together.

Fast-forward to today. Here I am, the proud founder of Dr. Michelle Marie Wealth Coaching, LLC. Every step of this journey has been guided by signs, opportunities, and incredible people, who have crossed my path. It's been a series of moments that have shaped my path and continue to guide me each day.

You know what brings me the greatest joy in all of this? Seeing the transformation in every client I work with. Each one walks away with a newfound sense of peace and clarity, knowing and seeing that they can achieve financial independence and become debt-free. That's what it's all about for me—empowering others and helping them find that inner strength to take control of their financial future.

Experiencing these moments of mentorship, working alongside Tamra, and witnessing the transformation of my clients have been the fuel that keeps me going. They have led me to where I am today, and they continue to guide me on this incredible journey.

So, if you're wondering how I ended up as an entrepreneur, it's a story of synchronicity, support, and a deep desire to make a positive impact. I am forever grateful for the amazing people who have come into my life and for the signs that have guided me along the way. It's a journey filled with joy, growth, and endless possibilities.

What does being a joy-full entrepreneur mean to you and how is this emphasized in your daily life?

Being a joy-full entrepreneur might not be as simple as it seems. Loving Jesus and running a business don't automatically guarantee joy. So let's explore this further. *Joy*, according to Merriam-Webster, stems from well-being, success, and anticipation of fulfilling our desires. And when we say *full*, it means enjoying all the privileges and characteristics that come with it. But how do we truly experience this all-encompassing joy?

Well, Romans 15:13 holds the answer: "May the God of hope fill you with all joy and peace as you trust in him, so that you may overflow with hope by the power of the Holy Spirit." That's the key! As I navigate my entrepreneurial journey each day, my trust in God becomes paramount.

Now this doesn't mean everything will go exactly as planned or that every pitch will be met with a resounding "yes." It means entrusting every action, consultation, and social media post to God. Being a joy-full entrepreneur means staying focused, maintaining a positive perspective, praying throughout the process, and seeking divine guidance—even when my desires may lead me elsewhere. It means making a conscious decision to keep going and not giving up when faced with challenges.

Each day I have the privilege of sharing God's wisdom with others and helping them avoid the financial pitfalls I once encountered. And let me tell you, that brings me immense joy and fulfillment. It fills my cup, leaving me satisfied and content.

Being a joy-full entrepreneur isn't solely about loving Jesus and integrating faith into my business. It's about wholeheartedly trusting Him, staying positive, and making a difference in the lives of others. That's where genuine joy resides, and that's what motivates me every single day.

Who biblically has been a consistent mentor in your pursuit of excellence as an entrepreneur? What are their unique character traits and how have they modeled being a joy-full entrepreneur well?

Let me tell you about someone who has been a consistent mentor in my pursuit of excellence as an entrepreneur—Tamra Andress. She has not only been a faith-based business coach but also an inspiration to me through her own hills and valleys. It's incredible to see how she navigated those challenges while staying true to her faith.

What really struck me about Tamra was her character. She embodies traits like humility, honesty, faithfulness, courage, dedication, and patience. These qualities have served as a model for me as I strive to be a joy-full entrepreneur. I've seen how she pushed through the hard times and how she sometimes had to say no to good opportunities because she knew that something greater was on the horizon. Her dedication to her calling as a faith-filled entrepreneur, despite the world urging her to do things differently, has been truly instrumental in guiding my own journey. And here's the incredible part—she probably didn't even realize it!

I truly believe that as female entrepreneurs, we embody the essence of Proverbs 31 women. And for me, Tamra is a shining example of that. She exemplifies what it means to pursue excellence, to walk in faith, and to make a difference in the lives of others. Her journey has inspired me to keep pushing forward, even when faced with challenges and doubts.

Having Tamra as a mentor has been an incredible blessing. Her God-given wisdom, steadfast encouragement, and genuine faith walk have had a profound impact on my own entrepreneurial path. She has shown me that it's possible to be a joy-full entrepreneur and to thrive in the business world while staying true to my beliefs and values.

I am grateful for the lessons I've learned from Tamra and the guidance she has provided, even unknowingly. She has helped shape my perspective on what it means to be a successful entrepreneur not just in terms of financial gain but in living out a purpose-driven life. I am inspired to follow in her footsteps, to be courageous, and to embrace the journey with joy and faith.

Tamra, thank you for being a consistent mentor and for being an incredible example of what it means to be a Proverbs 31 woman. Your impact on my life and my entrepreneurial journey is immeasurable.

What has been your biggest challenge or trial in keeping your joy as an entrepreneur and leader?

What's the biggest challenge in keeping my joy as an entrepreneur and leader, you ask? It's the process itself. Setting up a business, building systems, staying consistent, and staying the course have been quite the adventure. But you know what? They've also been the greatest reward.

Building a business from scratch is no walk in the park. It takes dedication, hard work, and loads of resilience. There were times when I felt overwhelmed and questioned if I could continue. But those challenges, tough as they were, shaped me. They pushed me to tap into a wellspring of determination I didn't even know existed.

Not only did these challenges shape me as an entrepreneur, but they also fueled my growth as a leader. They compelled me to step up, become more charismatic, and truly inspire others. After all, how can I help others overcome their financial hurdles if I can't conquer my own as a coach?

Every "no," every low-visibility post, and every late-night work session tested my resolve. But you know what? They reminded me of Jesus during His ministry. Despite facing immense tribulations, He conquered the world (John 16:33). While my journey can't compare to His, this knowledge gives me courage and hope to pursue my calling.

And you know what brings me joy every single day? My refusal to give up. I keep pushing forward, knowing that with each step, I grow stronger, more resilient, and closer to my goals. The process may be challenging, but within it lies the greatest rewards. The joy I feel isn't fleeting; it's a profound sense of fulfillment that comes from living out my purpose.

So, my friend, if you're facing challenges in your own entrepreneurial journey, remember that it's in the process where you'll find strength, courage, and resilience. Embrace the journey, keep your eyes on the prize, and never lose sight of the joy that comes from pursuing your calling. Just like me, you have the power to conquer your hurdles and discover joy in the midst of it all.

What wisdom or encouragement would you give someone who has never blended their faith and business strategy as one? How has it aided in your profitability?

First things first, let's talk about prayer. It's not just some boring ritual—it's a supercharged tool in your entrepreneurial journey. Take time to seek God's guidance, surrender those plans of yours, and trust in His divine wisdom. Believe me, He's got some amazing insights to offer!

Next, build your business on a solid foundation. Implementing effective systems is the name of the game. Make sure they reflect your integrity, core values, and mission. Dedicate yourself wholeheartedly to your vision because success often requires persistence, hard work, and unwavering dedication. You've got this!

But, hey, you don't have to go at it alone. Having a mentor or coach by your side is like having a secret weapon. They'll provide guidance, support, and accountability. And don't forget about your cheerleading squad—surround yourself with friends, family, and fellow believers who will uplift you in prayer. Their intercession is like a turbo boost for your journey!

Now here's a pro-tip: when things get exciting and challenging during times of transition and growth, turn up the volume on your prayer life. These moments can be a bit overwhelming, and the world might try to pull you in different directions. But by focusing on prayer and seeking God's guidance, you'll stay on the right path and make decisions that align with His awesome plans for you.

Stay humble, my friend. It's important to ask for help and feedback along the way. None of us have all the answers (sorry, not even me). Embrace your mistakes, own up to them, and use them as opportunities for growth. Authenticity and vulnerability are like magnets that draw respect from your followers and clients.

Let's wrap this up with a dose of Scripture that'll make your heart soar. Proverbs 3:5–6 says, "Trust in the Lord with all your heart … He will make your paths straight." Isn't that awesome? So go ahead and embrace the power of prayer, rock those effective systems, and stay dedicated, patient, and determined. Trust that God is guiding you every step of the way.

Closing Thoughts

Remember, my friend, you have been called to greatness as a joy-full entrepreneur. Embrace the process, lean on your faith, and step boldly into the extraordinary life that awaits you. May you experience abundant blessings and the fulfillment of your deepest desires. Keep shining your light and inspiring others as you walk the path of faith-filled entrepreneurship.

I invite you to connect with me on social media, where I share further insights, encouragement, and resources. You can find me on Instagram and Facebook at @dr.michellemarie. For more information about my work and how I can support you on your financial journey, visit my website at drmichellemarie.com.

Let your light so shine before men, that they may see your good works, and glorify your Father which is in heaven.

Matthew 5:16.

Kathryn McAdam

Hello, I'm Kathryn J. McAdam, a nurse practitioner, worship leader, Christian minister, and podcast host who also has experienced the heartache of marriage to a drug addict, divorce, and homelessness. I have worked for over fifteen years in the medical field and am now a co-owner of a solar grids company with my husband, Joseph McAdam.

Most of all, I am an overcomer who can completely understand what you are going through and speak life into your situation, bringing hope and encouragement that you, too, can live a life of unstoppable joy!

I'm not here to give you pat answers or cliché scripture verses. I am here to honestly share with you the mindset hurdles and the spiritual and emotional barriers I had to overcome on my journey to becoming a "comeback queen."

My deepest desire is that as I share my story, you will find unstoppable joy as well!

Chapter 11
The Unstoppable Joy-Filled Entrepreneur

Would you describe your entrepreneurial adventure as a solution, a sign, or a wonder based on your personal testimony and experience? Explain.

I would describe my entrepreneurial adventure as a sign.

My journey as an entrepreneur started years ago, when I was a teen-ager. As a gifted, competitive swimmer, I was always in the water. So naturally, I ended up becoming a lifeguard and certified swim instructor. I loved teaching and soon started my own business offering private swim lessons to children in my little town. I loved being able to set my own hours and make a great wage doing something I enjoyed. I always tithed off my earnings and felt God's hand as I helped several who had near drowning experiences overcome their fears of the water.

I have always been a risk-taker and bold about my faith, but it wasn't until my faith was tested that I really knew God personally …

My faith in God originated with my parents. One night, when I was about four years old, my mother was saying prayers with one of my sisters in the bed next to mine. She began explaining the way of salvation and how to be sure you have a home in heaven. As she was asking my older sister if she wanted to be sure of this, I called out, "Me too; I want a home in heaven!"

I am second to the last of my parents' eight children. But even though I grew up in a household of ten, I always felt a little lost and alone. I was very outspoken and strong-willed. This did not go over well with authoritarian parents who expected their children to obey without question. I heard repeatedly what a bad child I was and how they never had as much trouble with the other kids as they had with me. No doubt, with my boldness, it was true. And as a result, my defiance often found the end of the rod of correction.

I have come to realize over the years that my love language is quality time, but with eight children to care for, quality time was something my parents had very little of. Eventually, the hurtful words and a lack of nurturing time left me feeling unloved and unlovely. This sense of rejection by my parents wreaked havoc on my self-esteem and spilled into my relationship with God.

When I was in grade school, my mother gave me a bookmark with my name, my name's meaning, and a scripture written on it. The bookmark stated that my name, Katherine, meant *pure*, and the scripture read "And the Pure in heart shall see God." I knew Jesus as my Savior and remember thinking, "If only I could be pure in my heart, I could see God!" But though I had accepted Christ very young, I had never felt worthy or good. And as a result, my next thought was that my little heart was not pure and that seeing God was only a lofty dream.

My relationship with my parents continued to crumble into high school. I was a good student, active in my youth group, didn't drink or do drugs, helped with the housework and chores, worked to earn money for college, visited the elderly in a nearby nursing home, etc., but still my parents seemed to reject me. Thankfully, I found comfort in Psalm 27:10 (AMP), which says, "Although my father and my mother have abandoned me, Yet the Lord will take me up [adopt me as His child]."

I knew God loved me, but I felt so rejected by my parents that, when I met my first love, I soaked up his love and attention like a dried-out old sponge. This was a recipe for disaster. He was the pastor's son, and we were both youth-group leaders. Ecstatic that someone could love me, I was head over heels and quickly lost all sense of boundaries. Stolen glances soon led to more, and I lost my virginity. I knew better, and the guilt was crushing.

By God's grace, after two years of dating, things came to a screeching halt. My boyfriend decided he didn't love me and walked away. Many of our mutual youth-group friends quit talking to me as well. I was devastated. I had not told anyone about what had happened between us, and the devil tormented me. I wondered what man would ever love me now that I was "damaged goods." I quit eating and became severely depressed. I asked my parents if I could go to counseling, but they refused to let me go. Unable to sleep, I began memorizing scripture to help me through the nights. I clung to God and cried myself to sleep for months. My sin and the acute pain of rejection broke me. God truly became my refuge as I spent hours in daily praise, prayer, and Bible study.

Several months later, as I was lifeguarding early in the morning, I began doubting God's goodness. I had thought that if I gave Him my all, spent time with Him in His Word and prayer, and changed my ways, He would put my relationships back together. Nothing had changed. I felt more alone than ever.

So on that cold, snowy morning, as I sat in the dimly lit pool area, I decided that God was not real, and I was no longer a Christian. I had given God everything, turned my life upside down and sought Him with my whole being, and yet it didn't seem He was doing anything for me. Nothing was changing for the better.

In anger, I told God I didn't believe in Him anymore. I had turned my life over to Him, and He wasn't doing anything for me, so He must not be real. I rose and walked away from where I had been sitting thinking, "I'm not a Christian anymore; there is no right or wrong; I can do whatever I want ... drink, drugs, sex. Not that I want to do those things, but they are not wrong anymore." The thought of not being a Christian was so foreign to me. I had known Christ ever since I could remember. This new life was going to be very different, or so I thought. I walked away from my Bible and the little desk on which it sat that morning, and in my heart, I was walking away from God.

No sooner had I sat down at the other end of the pool area than a little old lady came walking towards me. She wore a one-piece skirted swimsuit, bathing cap, and a pair of oversized glasses. As I saw her near the kickboard bin, I thought, "Oh, get your own kickboard, lady." But she just kept walking, rounded the end of the pool, and came right up to me. Glasses on the bridge of her nose, curls peeking below her bathing cap, she looked me straight in the eye and said, "I was swimming, and God told me to come over here and tell you that He loves you." Stunned, I nearly fell off my seat. As I began to cry, she told me she had been praying for me and wanted to let me know that whatever I was going through, God was there, and He loved me. All I could think was, "He just won't let me go—not for a minute." He had sent her to tell me He loved me the very minute I was rebuking HIM. From that time forward, my faith in Christ was mine. It was not the faith I learned in Sunday school or heard my parents speak of. God was *real*, and He loved a messed up sinner like me!

Since that time, God has been my Rock and my *joy*. My journey with Christ truly began that day. Since then, I have followed Him to far corners of the globe ministering to hundreds through music and testimony and individually at the side of a sickbed in hospital rooms. I have overcome heartache, having a critically-ill child, abuse, divorce, financial ruin, and homelessness. And I have finally found my way back to becoming a Christian entrepreneur. My entrepreneurial journey is a sign of God's ability to bring about blessing and joy from the most tragic of circumstances. It is also a sign that God never stops calling us to a higher level. All for His glory, He has redeemed my story and blessed me beyond measure, when life had counted me out.

What Christ-like solutions have you discovered that make your day-to-day business manageable and fruitful?

My husband and I start each day in prayer. We thank God for the many blessings He has given us and ask Him to show us what He has for us to do each day. We ask for His divine guidance and assistance to accomplish the tasks that lie before us. Knowing that God is ultimately in control allows us to have peace when things do not seem to be going our way. Just like Joseph from the Old Testament, when our road does not look like the one we planned, we trust that God will work all things out for our good. Delays and disappointments often open doors for divine appointments and chance meetings that further God's plans in business and our lives. Because we have entrusted our day to Him, things that used to upset us now bring excitement about what God might be orchestrating.

What signs have been given to you along the way that have led you to say yes to exploring and activating your entrepreneurial spirit?

My husband Joe is the sign that was given to lead me to say yes to becoming an entrepreneur. He has also been instrumental in me opening up to share my story and venturing out as a solar franchise co-owner and sales person. He has the gift of helps and a deep desire to serve. He is a visionary and is always way ahead of me, signing me up for meetings with publishers and speaking events.

You see, fifteen years ago I found myself homeless with my three kids as we fled from my then drug addicted, ex-husband. After nearly ten years of marriage and multiple drug treatment programs, my ex-husband had also become abusive. I am so grateful for my sister and her husband who took us in until we could get back on our feet. At the time, I had nine months left of nursing school, and I commuted two hours to class. I pressed through and graduated with honors.

But years of being abused mentally, emotionally, and physically had taken its toll on me. Not only was I financially ruined, I was questioning if I could even hear from God. I spent years in therapy and struggled through raising my kids alone. Little by little, with God's help, I began to rebuild my life with my kids. I eventually completed my master's degree in nursing and now work part-time as a nurse practitioner and a co-owner of a solar franchise with my new husband, Joe. When I first shared my story with Joe, he was amazed by my strength and faith in God and has been encouraging me to share my story with others ever since. My first marriage was so awful that I knew if I ever were to get married again, it would have to be an amazing relationship. And that's exactly what I have found in Joe. He has also been through a great deal, but he just keeps moving forward with a smile on his face and a great attitude. His positive outlook and determination encourage me every day. He is the sign that I needed to get me to step out and share my story, start a podcast, and sell solar. Not only has he encouraged me to do all these things, but he has stood beside me and helped me with all the technical issues along the way. When I have felt like quitting, he has encouraged me to press on and not become weary in well-doing. He is the sign of God's goodness in my life and a reminder that God has great plans for me, plans to bless and prosper me.

Who biblically has been a consistent mentor in your pursuit of excellence as an entrepreneur? What are their unique character traits and how have they modeled being a joy-full entrepreneur well?

Joseph is the one biblical "mentor" that I have continually gleaned from through the years. His example of staying consistent in his pursuit of excellence, even in the most challenging and humbling situations, has inspired me over the years. As I have faced seemingly insurmountable difficulties, remembering that God will use everything that happens in our lives for good has encouraged me to be at peace in the midst of trials. The example of Joseph's story of consistency and how God used the trials he went through to position him for greatness has brought me hope knowing that God is in control. Even when he was sold into slavery, Joseph didn't let that stop him. While a slave in Potiphar's house, he became the most trusted servant. When he was falsely accused of rape by Potiphar's wife and sent to jail, he didn't sink down into self-pity and despair. Instead, he excelled as a leader and was put in charge of the other prisoners. To have moved up and been promoted in these challenging situations, he must have kept his calm, stayed positive, and operated in divine wisdom. His faith and courage under fire could only have come from a deep relationship with God. He knew who he was and who was ultimately in control of his life. He persevered through seventeen years of trial and testing with consistent integrity before that one day when he was asked to go before the king. His life changed in a moment as he went from the prison to the palace to interpret the king's dream and then offer advice on how to manage the situation. After years of serving faithfully, Joseph was promoted to manager of all the food stores of the land. I have faced seemingly insurmountable situations, financial ruin, false accusations, homelessness, and single parenthood over the last few decades of my life. Like Joseph, these trials have been the testing ground of my character. The lessons I have learned have instilled in me a tenacious faith and dependence on God. I have had the honor to watch as my story has encouraged and brought hope to so many over the years. I can truly say as Joseph did, "What was meant for evil against me, God meant for good."

What has been your biggest challenge or trial in keeping your joy as an entrepreneur and leader?

Honest people trust others to be honest as well. Be it naivety or ignorance, we want to believe the best of people. Unfortunately, people do not always have your best interests at heart. I have had the challenge of people using us for their own gain or promising things and not delivering. Remembering to forgive others quickly and not holding grudges have been key to keeping my joy as an entrepreneur.

How has your faith been sharpened as an entrepreneur?

My faith has been sharpened, as I have had to learn to trust God when I am not seeing results from my labor. It can be discouraging to work so hard and spend hours perfecting and packaging a certain project—all while having a sense of God's leading—only to have it flop. As things move slowly or seem to have screeched to a halt, I am brought to my knees in prayer. I am reminded to seek first God's kingdom and His righteousness and all these things will be added as well. I try to make sure that I am seeking Him and not just His hand of blessing. God is more interested in our character and our having a right relationship with Him than He is in our temporary happiness or success in business. His plans are all about the long game.

Closing Thoughts

If your eyes have landed on these pages of mine, then you must be searching for something. Be it encouragement, inspiration, or hope, you were meant to be here at this moment, reading these words. Whatever you are going through, please know that you are not alone. God is there with you. He is good, He loves you, and He can be trusted. Your path may not be easy, and there will be days that you may wrestle with Him, but keep asking, keep seeking, keep knocking! Do not give up! In the end, He will bless you. I know, I've been there. If He did it for me, He will certainly do it for you! I believe that you have come across my story for a reason. Through Unstoppable Joy, I offer courses, coaching, and communities. To find out more and to keep up-to-date on all the happenings go to unstoppable-joy.com/.

Thanks for reading!

Be Blessed,
Kathryn

I press toward the goal for the prize of the upward call of God in Christ Jesus

Philippians 3:14.

Natalie Petroskey

Natalie, a.k.a. Coach Nat, is a multi-talented individual, juggling roles as a wife, mother, entrepreneur, and coach. Her success includes owning four businesses: Legacy Lacrosse, Milestone Manor, Legacy Leaders Academy, and Reliance Enterprises. Her primary gifts are coaching and *building*, and she has been guiding and mentoring others for over fifteen years. With coaching as an anointing, Coach Nat loves to *build* teams and bring people together to do extraordinary things!

She understands firsthand what it is to *build* and empower in business, on the field, and in people. She grew her first business to six figures in the first six months! In the world of sports, she has won three championships—one as a player and two as a head coach, showcasing her tenacity and winning mindset.

Faith is her cornerstone, and all things flow from that. Natalie also believes that discipleship is not only a declaration but a *built* relationship. She believes in order to show the love of Jesus you must bless, fellowship, minister, and then proclaim the kingdom; in that order!

Her most important role is being a wife to the love of her life, Steve, and a mama to her precious boys, Maximus (9), Marcus (7), and Maverick (4).

Chapter 12
Building on a Rock

Would you describe your entrepreneurial adventure as a solution, a sign, or a wonder based on your personal testimony and experience? Explain.

My entrepreneurial adventure began like most, fulfilling a need (solution) for the customers in my marketplace. Since being on the path of entrepreneurship, I have realized that God wants it to be a sign AND a wonder as well. We can't put God in a box, even though we really do try. And I believe we try so that we might understand everything that He is doing. But once we realize that we were never supposed to understand it all, we are able to move in freedom with Him and be used as His living water to the people we were called to serve … to be a solution, to be a sign for others, and to be a wonder.

As an owner of businesses, solutions are needed every day to tackle, overcome, and advance whatever it is you are doing in that specific market. But when you are a kingdom entrepreneur, your scope goes beyond the business in the natural, and you start to reach for the signs and wonders in the supernatural. And even if you don't do that, God will. God called me out and began my journey all the way back when I was nineteen. During that difficult year, I had come to the revelation that nothing I did was in my control. During the second semester of my sophomore year of college, I was accused of plagiarism (found not guilty), I was sexually assaulted, and I was in a horrible car accident. On the corner of the intersection of that accident, I stood there physically unscathed but absolutely spiritually wrecked. As a successful collegiate athlete and a go-getter in my academics, most would not have known the downward spiral that the enemy had me on. That day, standing on the corner of an intersection, I got on my knees and wept and cried out to God. I gave my life to Jesus in that moment. We all like to talk about the defining moments in our life where God revealed Himself to us. And, yes, they do exist and are powerful testimonies, but His power and presence are also revealed in the many small moments throughout our day, when we can miss Him moving. When I look back on my life, I see those moments almost more clearly than the pivotal ones. And I am left with awe and wonder. My God was with me in that moment? In this place? Directing me this way? Yes!

So when I think about the entrepreneurial adventure, it really is just that—a constant, ever changing, and ever growing process of putting down what you thought it was all about and enjoying the beautiful moments where God says, no, do it this way, walk that way, show up in this way. All the while, you are left with all the signs and wonders around you that could only be orchestrated by God.

How do you allow the supernatural signs to direct your path, process, profit plan, and partnerships in business?

My first step in allowing God to move in my businesses is to give them to Him every day. Sometimes I have to give them to Him more than once in the day. When you are a believer, you posture and approach your business and your customers/clients differently. I will be the first to say I do not have this mastered, and it is a continual refinement. It has to be.

I am not necessarily a fan of the phrase "bigger levels, bigger devils" because that alludes to the enemy being bigger, and that is just not true. But do I believe the pressure and the stakes can feel higher as you become bigger and more successful? Unequivocally, yes! That is why it is absolutely imperative to lay our own lives down and pick up the cross. We pray a lot about God blessing us. But when you lay your life and business at the foot of the cross and give it to Him, it becomes God's, and by default, it is blessed! How simple, right?

I believe deeply that once you hand it to Him, the path, process, profit, and right people will come. I have witnessed it. I also understand there is an enemy that will try to steal, kill, and destroy the very thing that is blessed. But he can't touch God. And that is why I *have* to give up everything to God. It is the only way to protect and steward what He has given me. There is no other way.

The word *success* has been manipulated by that very same enemy. So just like I lay down my life and my businesses at God's feet, I also have to lay down what I think success is—what the world says it is. And this is a constant battle, the tug and pull of what the world says I need to do and what God is telling me to do. We are in the world, but we are not of it. And sometimes, standing out and doing things that don't make sense to others is exactly what God is asking us to do. The one thing God told me when He placed me in the marketplace was: "You will either be pulled towards me or away from me. You must always choose the things that pull you towards me, and say no to the things that pull you away." That has been the most important business advice I have ever received, and it was from God.

The last thing I will say is that when you do give it to God, He works at a supernatural pace that is almost impossible to keep up with. But this does not equate with busy, overloaded, stressed, or hustling. It is actually effortless … but fast!! When I have truly yielded my businesses to Him, I know that I better be ready. I better be healthy and strong—mind, body, spirit. Following God is so fantastic but also very overwhelming … in the most beautiful way! God always makes a way. *Always*! He has always made a way for me in my businesses and life, even if it was at the last moment. But I wouldn't want it any other way.

Who biblically has been a consistent mentor in your pursuit of excellence as an entrepreneur? What are their unique character traits and how have they modeled being a joy-full entrepreneur well?

There are three mentors from the Bible that I always lean on. Joseph, King Solomon, and King David. The ultimate mentor, however, is Jesus, and I do not want to miss giving Him the most deserving praises. There are far too many lessons He has taught me in my life. But the Bible is the Word, and the Word is God, so I know He believes these people to be mentors to me as well.

Joseph has taught me so much about the anointing from God and his appointment in that anointing. He has also taught me that God's plan for your life will *not* look like what you thought it would but to find peace and *joy* in that space regardless. He shows us that when God's plan for us goes against the world, God will still get what He wants in the end. Our appointing never comes at the same time as our anointing. He has to nurture us and teach us and guide us to that very place.

King Solomon has reminded me and convicted me that our giftings and blessings are so we can be a gift and a blessing to the people we are called to serve. Of course God cares about me, but I also realize that everything He has given me is so that I can give that to the people He has commissioned me to serve. The living waters that flow through us are exactly that … *through* us. We will be blessed by being a blessing. King Solomon understood that the only way he could be the king God anointed him to be was to gain as much wisdom as possible. And because the one thing he asked from God had nothing to do with him, God gave him supernatural wisdom and blessed King Solomon with all the riches and abundance. The goal wasn't to be successful. The goal was to be a blessing!

King David has taught me that my personal relationship with God is absolutely imperative. It is not an option. My relationship with Him is the most important relationship I will ever have, and realizing that has given me a whole other perspective about life and what God has for me. I did not grow up journaling or having a diary. As my walk with the Lord goes deeper, however, I understand the importance of allowing God to move through my thoughts and words—my personal Psalms. The relationship God had with King David is the same relationship He wants with me. That is powerful.

I have learned a lot from these three men of God on how to posture and also how to walk in authority—on my knees and face. The world will want to tear you down, deceive you, enslave you, and even try and kill you. But what God promises through these three people is that, when you know the kingdom perspective and follow Him, you will be blessed so that you can serve—Servant Leadership. My prayer when I want or "need" something is: "God, show me where this will bless the people I am called to serve. If it doesn't, change my heart. Block the enemy from manipulating my flesh to want desires that are not yours." Money and abundance are not evil; the love of the things not of God is. We must always consider the heart posture …

Joseph never asked to have the keys to the kingdom. And that is why he did. King Solomon never asked for riches and a life of abundance, but he received more than he could have ever asked for because his heart pleased God. King David was a boy when God anointed him. He grew up always seeking God and is known for his deep love for God. A man after God's heart. All of them served the very people God anointed them to serve—not with perfection but with God as the center.

What has been your biggest challenge or trial in keeping your joy as an entrepreneur and leader?

My biggest challenge is being misunderstood—not by the world but by fellow believers. We tend to think the enemy is this big dragon we can see with both eyes wide open. But he is a master schemer and manipulator. As believers, we are not immune to this, but we have the Holy Spirit, and so we lean on discernment. The enemy, however, can be insidious and in the most unlikely places. I am well aware that this is not a comfortable answer, but I do believe it will bring comfort and resonate with most believers. This is why we need a constant refinement and understanding that our prayers for those who misunderstand us can transform. The same enemy who walks to and fro on the earth is the same enemy who wants to place himself right in the middle of the pulpit and tear the Ekklesia apart … if we let him.

Leadership and entrepreneurship are almost synonymous. Well, at least I believe you can't be an entrepreneur without being a leader. And if you aren't a leader, you will learn how very quickly. So let's focus on the word *leader*. The Bible describes successful leaders as honoring and surrendering to God's authority, serving others, and caring for those they serve. And the Bible is pretty bold about leaders who do the opposite and lead people astray and into the darkness. Matthew 18:6 (NKJV) says, "But whoever causes one of these little ones who believe in Me to sin, it would be better for him if a millstone were hung around his neck, and he were drowned in the depth of the sea." This verse makes an important point: as a leader, you can lead people to God, or you can lead them away. That is why it also tells us to pray for our leaders. 1 Timothy 2:1–2 says, "I urge, then, first of all, that petitions, prayers, intercession and thanksgiving be made for all people—for kings and all those in authority, that we may live peaceful and quiet lives in all godliness and holiness." This is no easy feat. In the inspirational movie Spiderman (insert wink), Aunt May says, "With great power comes great responsibility." Or if we keep it biblical, which is better, of course, Luke 12:48 says, "But the one who does not know and does things deserving punishment will be beaten with few blows. From everyone who has been given much, much will be demanded; and from the one who has been entrusted with much, much more will be asked." That is leadership. So if the enemy can take out the leader who is leading many, he can affect the masses.

So what does this have to do with being misunderstood by fellow believers? Everything. Once you have stepped into the place of leadership, it is inevitable that words and beliefs that are false will arise. Anyone in leadership in business, ministry, family, etc. understands that a target will always be on their back. We are not to wear that with offense or discord.

And we also don't wear that as a badge of honor. We have to understand who the real enemy is. And this can be hard when the arrows are coming from our brothers and/or sisters. It can hurt. It can be downright painful—But God.

In my walk and as an entrepreneur, it has been imperative that I understand the real enemy and the deceit and wickedness he wants to create—and to not placate it. You posture as a leader on your knees, you pray for the leaders leading you, and you give the rest of it to God. I have also had to learn deeply that you will never be fully understood. I say again … you will never be fully understood. God is our true source of confidence and affirmation.

How has your faith been sharpened as an entrepreneur?

Have you ever heard of the famous quote by Theodore Roosevelt, from his speech "Man in the Arena?" Let me share it:

> It is not the critic who counts; not the man who points out how the strong man stumbles, or where the doer of deeds could have done them better. The credit belongs to the man who is actually in the arena, whose face is marred by dust and sweat and blood; who strives valiantly; who errs, who comes short again and again, because there is no effort without error and shortcoming; but who does actually strive to do the deeds; who knows great enthusiasms, the great devotions; who spends himself in a worthy cause; who at the best knows in the end the triumph of high achievement, and who at the worst, if he fails, at least fails while daring greatly, so that his place shall never be with those cold and timid souls who neither know victory nor defeat.

In entrepreneurship, you are placed in the arena. Whether or not you want the fights that come your way, you will face them. The same goes with all the victories! But with all the courage and strength and effort, there is no way you can do it without having faith. My faith and relationship with God are a direct result of my entrepreneurial journey. In every relationship, it's the adversity you go through that builds deeper connection. Entrepreneurship is one of the scariest and most rewarding things I have ever done. I thank God every day for giving me the heart to step in the arena—not for the victories but because it has given me a deeper faith and *love* for God.

What wisdom or encouragement would you give someone who has never blended their faith and business strategy as one? How has it aided in your profitability?

Everything good we have in this life has always been God's, even our businesses ... *especially* our businesses! It is not whether we want to give them to God; It is whether we want to allow God to move in them. He wants us to invite Him into our lives. He wants to work *with* us. The quicker we understand this, the more fruitful and fulfilling our lives will be. On those days I haven't allowed Him in, I picture Him as a patient Father, watching me struggle to lift a heavy box or unravel a knotted ball of yarn. And He is just waiting for me to say, "Can you help me with this?!" And He says, "Sure!" This is in life, and it is absolutely in our businesses. We think we do it all in our own strength and understanding. Meanwhile, our Father has the *full* understanding and the exponential strength needed. Why wouldn't we call upon Him? Because of our flesh. Because of our sin.

We can talk about finances and profits, business successes, resources, and partnerships, but I have learned that once you realize that God wants to be at the center of it all, He will transform everything! I have seen the direct impact of doing things *my* way and watching productivity slow down. I have also seen what God's way looks like, and it has been something I never could have imagined. It doesn't always look like that or feel like that at the moment. But when you release everything to Him, even the timing of things, just wait and be expectant. He will change the whole game. I once heard that we are all just playing checkers while God is playing the biggest game of chess, and He has already called checkmate! Wow! Talk about humbling yourself. I want the God of Abraham, the God of Moses, the God of Solomon, the God of David, the God of Esther, the God of Mary to be in control of my business. When you shift that massive perspective, there is no other way to conduct your life or your business!

Closing Thoughts

There is a constant theme over my life. I am a builder. I love to build teams, businesses, and people—most importantly, people. That is the coach in me. I see people. I see them the way God sees them. I also understand that great teams and great companies don't build themselves. That takes people! If I had it my way, I would have daily meetings with the people in my life! Community and fellowship are a huge part of my heart and what lights me up is building things together! God gave me the heart and gifts to be a builder but not without Him. He is the foundation. He is the Rock! And as long as we remember that, we will build greatness together.

But the one who always listens to me will live undisturbed in a heavenly peace. Free from fear, confident and courageous, that one will rest unafraid and sheltered from the storms of life

Proverbs 1:33, TPT.

Wendy Rhodes

Hello, I'm Wendy Rhodes, the Founder of Hearth & Home Property Solutions, LLC. With a passion for transforming old houses into beautiful homes, I strive to create spaces where people can live their best lives. I hold a Bachelor's Degree in Business Administration, and prior to embarking on my journey as an entrepreneur, I gained valuable experience working in a corporate environment. When I'm not working, I enjoy spending time with my family and traveling.

Chapter 13
Just Follow the Blueprint!

Would you describe your entrepreneurial adventure as a solution, a sign, or a wonder based on your personal testimony and experience? Explain.

I believe my business is a wonder. Why? Because it is an extension of me, of who I am, and what God has called me to do. Psalms 139:14 says, "I am fearfully and wonderfully made." When I stop to think about this verse, I think about the level of detail God has gone into to create my body—how everything works together simply to breathe, to walk, to talk, to think, to reason. This didn't just happen; I am created and designed by God Himself. He knew me before I was formed in my mother's womb. He knew me, He thought of me, and He created me. He said this world needs a Wendy, and she will look like this, walk like this, and talk like this with her southern accent sprinkled in. But these comprise only the outer shell. On the inside, I am made up of cells, DNA, blood vessels, and so many other things that are in and of themselves miraculously made. But beyond that, I have feelings and emotions and thoughts that have the power to shape who I am, where I go, what I accomplish, and what my future looks like. I have been given the keys to unlock all of the potential God designed for me to walk in—not just walk in but thrive in! He has a plan for each of us, and it is our responsibility to find, discover, and pursue what He created us to do. Some people are blessed to be naturally talented at certain things, such as singing, playing an instrument, teaching, or preaching. Others are uncertain about what their gifts and talents are. Or maybe they know but choose not to pursue them because of expectations others have placed on them, like the accountant who loves playing the guitar or the doctor who would rather be in the business world or the factory worker who would rather be serving on a mission field. God has put inside each one of us a desire to do something—something He created us to do. What is your passion? Find it, follow it, and there you will find your purpose.

My passion is real estate. I love helping people who have found themselves in difficult situations get out of that place and get a fresh start. They find themselves in these situations because life happened. Maybe they were laid off from their job, they are getting divorced, or sickness has prevented them from being able to work, and they can no longer afford their home. I provide a way out. What I offer is not for everyone but only for a certain few. These people feel stuck in their circumstances. Most of the houses I have purchased have fallen into disrepair. The owners don't have the money or ability to make the repairs needed to get them top dollar. Many are ashamed and embarrassed by where they are in life and the state their homes are in. I'm the easy button for them. I buy houses "as is." They can close the door, walk away, and never look back. It gives them a sense of relief, a chance to begin again ... just like when someone finds Jesus. He takes all of the messes that we've made in life—our sin, our shame, our brokenness—and makes it all brand new. No judgment. He takes us as we are and says, "You are mine, and I love you." We don't have to change for Him to accept us. He created us, He knows us, He loves us, and He has a plan and purpose for each of us. We just have to trust Him. If we earnestly seek Him, He will give us the desires of our heart. He is a good Father who wants to give us good things, starting with a renewed spirit. Remember, He made us, and He knows us better than we know ourselves. "For He chose us in Him before the creation of the world to be holy and blameless in His sight" (Eph. 1:4). So if He knew us before the world began, don't you think He still knows you now? Of course He does! And He has a purpose for you—just like He does for me! God blows my mind on the regular! He opens doors for me. He leads me to those who need help and brings the people that I need to do business with into my life. Contractors, attorneys, real estate agents, insurance agents, bankers, everyday people … He brings the people I need and people that need me to make this business succeed. Just as I am fearfully and wonderfully made, so is my business because it is my calling, my purpose, and an extension of me.

What Christ-like solutions have you discovered that make your day-to-day business manageable and fruitful?

The Christ-like solution I have found is love and compassion for others. I often find myself in the homes of people who are hurting. They are hurting because of something someone else has done or something they themselves have done or didn't do. Life happens. Marriages fail, we make bad choices, loved ones pass away, and employers downsize. When bad things happen, people respond in different ways. Some can muddle through and come out stronger, and some spiral downward and find themselves stuck. My purpose is to offer a helping hand to those who are stuck, to push back the overgrowth in their lives and allow light to come in, and to offer a ray of sunshine and hope to those who feel like there is no way out. Many choose not to take the help that is offered. Many choose to stay stuck and often find themselves with no place to go because their homes have been foreclosed on. I'm not saying I have the only answer to their problem; I'm just one option. I try to exhaust every avenue. I give options for those who want to stay in their home. Some of them are viable options and some of them are not. It just depends on the circumstances. My desire is always to help everyone I can.

As I mentioned before, God has a good plan for us. He wants us to enjoy our lives. He wants us to experience all He has for us. But to do that, we must make a decision to move. And I've learned through my own experience that not deciding is indeed making a decision. To decide means to determine, to settle, to commit to whatever it is. We choose a path and stick to it. You may have heard the saying "I'm sick and tired of being sick and tired." It's usually at that point a decision is made to do something different. Why? Because what we were doing wasn't working. We need to change the course, even if it's ever so slight. Just a one degree change in the flight plan will make the airplane arrive in a completely different location. Our choices, our decisions can move the needle. We can move it one degree or 180 degrees; the choice is ours. I choose to move the needle with love and compassion for those who are hurting and with hope for what seems like a hopeless situation.

What signs have been given to you along the way that have led you to say yes to exploring and activating your entrepreneurial spirit?

It's funny you should ask this question. I have always had a spirit of adventure and a willingness to take risks. I was a bit of a daredevil kid, always traipsing through the woods exploring, looking for that undiscovered treasure that would change my life forever. While I never found the treasure chest full of gold, what I found was golden. I found the spirit to break new ground, to conquer uncharted territory, to find that thing that would make the world a better place for everyone—the spirit of the entrepreneur. I was always curious, always optimistic, always believing that I could make a difference. Faith. Yeah, that's it! Faith that I had a purpose bigger than me.

It's ironic that in my early twenties I had a desire to learn real estate investing. But everyone around me convinced me it would never work; it was a scam! You had to have money to make money. I allowed all their fears and concerns to persuade me into not pursuing my passion. While I could kick myself for listening to them, I understand they were trying to protect me and keep me safe, to keep me from getting hurt or making a foolish decision. It didn't squash my entrepreneurial spirit, though. I just did other things instead. I tried my hand at so many things that didn't work. Some of these ventures included running a wall-cleaning business, selling rubber roof coatings, selling makeup with a multi-level marketing company, and selling insurance and other financial services (which ultimately landed me where I am today). I currently own an income tax preparation franchise and a real estate investing company that flips properties and has a rental portfolio. I finally made it full circle back to my passion. Real estate!

A number of the signs along the way pointed me back to real estate. Over the years, I owned a couple of rental properties, and my ex-husband and I flipped a foreclosed property that was across the street from where we lived. After my divorce, I dated a general contractor for five years who flipped some of the most dilapidated houses I had ever seen. Having been exposed to these kinds of real estate transactions in a safe way, I knew I could do it too. However, there were some pieces of the puzzle missing for me. I didn't know how to find the properties, and I didn't know how to pay for them. I surely didn't have a big pile of cash sitting around. So I invested in myself through coaching and mentorships and began learning as much as I could. And now, after just a couple of years, I have a real estate business on its way to making seven figures a year. God continues to open doors for me that blow my mind. I finally made it full circle and this is just the beginning. There's no time to take my foot off the gas because, as I accomplish great things, the vision and the dream keep expanding into even greater dreams and visions—visions to provide affordable housing, visions to provide housing for kids aging out of the foster care system, visions to provide housing for veterans and the elderly. Although these are still in the vision stage, I have no doubt that they will happen. It's not "if" but "when" because of the entrepreneurial spirit that God has given me. It's like Isaiah 40:31 (KJV) says, "But they that wait upon the Lord shall renew their strength; they shall mount up with wings as eagles; they shall run, and not be weary; and they shall walk, and not faint." So don't grow weary, and don't let anything or anyone keep you from the life God has designed for you. You have a purpose, a calling, a destiny!

How do you allow supernatural signs to direct your path, process, profit plan, and partnerships in business?

I love this question! I ask God for His help! I don't mean an overall blanket "help me, God" kind of prayer. I get down to the nitty gritty with God. When I have the opportunity to visit a property, I ask God for wisdom and insight. I ask for specific things, like "Do you want me to buy this house?" "How can I best help this seller?" "What do you think I should do with the property?" "Will you send me good, reliable contractors and others I can work with?" Time and time again, God answers my prayers. He gives me wisdom. He tells me what to do and how to do it—things I wouldn't know. For example, I had several flips going on, and I had another one about to start. I was feeling overwhelmed and asked God what to do. He told me to list the new property for sale with a realtor and at what price. I did, and it sold within a couple of days for over the asking price. Mind you, this was not a renovated house; it was a hot mess. This was such a blessing for me, and it was also a blessing for another flipper who was looking for his first house to renovate. It was a win-win.

God will lead me to people and properties that just blow my mind. I've acquired properties for a bargain because the owners were just tired of dealing with them. They have a broken-down house, and all they see is a mess. What I see is potential! I take that broken-down, neglected house and turn it into something beautiful—a home that someone else is willing to buy at a premium. I guess I love doing this so much because that's exactly what God did for me. He took my life, which was a broken-down, neglected mess and breathed new life into me. He restored my weary mind, body, and soul. He loved me back to life, the life He died to give me. My work is now a reflection of His love for me. He will do the same for you!

Who biblically has been a consistent mentor in your pursuit of excellence as an entrepreneur? What are their unique character traits and how have they modeled being a joy-full entrepreneur well?

This question is a little more difficult because there are so many real people with real problems who overcame in the Bible: Moses, who had a speech impediment, became a great leader; Esther, who was thrust into a marriage and a position of influence through her courage and boldness; Mary, the unwed mother who bravely carried her child despite the hardships and scorn she endured; and Jesus, let's not forget about the greatest man (God incarnate) who ever walked the earth! And how could Jesus not be my favorite mentor you ask? Oh, He is, but He is not the one I choose to write about today. For the purposes of this chapter, I have chosen to write about the businesswoman from Proverbs 31. As an entrepreneur, she has served me as a mentor and has had a huge impact on my life and my work.

The woman described in Proverbs 31 is the epitome of a joy-full entrepreneur. She was wise, confident, and generous. She was industrious. She was a real estate investor! "She considers a field and buys it …" (Proverbs 31:16). Yes!! That's what I'm talking about!! Not only that, with her profits she planted a vineyard. Can you say residual income? Furthermore, "She made linen garments and sold them and supplied the merchants with sashes" (Proverbs 31:24). Now we're talking about multiple streams of income. And because of the quality of her work, she was confident her products would sell. Verse 17 says she worked hard, she knew her strengths, and she capitalized on them. She carried herself as a successful, joy-full entrepreneur. She dressed for success because she wore fine linen and purple. What does it mean that she wore purple? It's not just the color. Purple dye in biblical times was very expensive. It was a very tedious and time-consuming process to collect purple dye, which was why it was so expensive. She was so successful that she wore the finest clothes. She knew her worth and value and proudly displayed the quality of her work in the clothes she made for herself and her family. She was also generous. Verse 20 says she opened her arms to the poor and extended her hands to the needy. She was blessed by hard work and wisdom and gladly shared with others. She had a heart of generosity. She loved her family and worked hard to provide for them, giving them the finest things. She had a great work ethic. She got up early and knocked out the things that needed to be done first—her quiet time, prayers, journaling, reading, exercising—and then she would start her day. Her priorities were set. She is a great role model and mentor for how I should pattern my day and how to live the life of a joy-full entrepreneur.

What has been your biggest challenge or trial in keeping your joy as an entrepreneur and leader?

Wow! Keeping your joy is a choice … a hard choice. While being an entrepreneur is very rewarding, it's not all fun and games. Sometimes you have to make hard decisions, decisions that affect others. And sometimes those decisions have negative impacts or repercussions that are unexpected. Things don't always go as planned. My biggest challenge to keeping my joy has been around the issue of control. And I admit to losing my joy over things that are beyond my control, like budgets being blown by some unexpected problem and timelines not being met causing a ripple effect for every task that falls in line behind it. Then there are people … Oh my goodness! It can be so frustrating when people do not do what they're supposed to do when they said they would do it—whether it's a seller, a buyer, a contractor, an attorney's office—or me. I want everyone and everything to fall in line with my plans, and when they don't, I can lose my joy. Stress, anxiety, frustrations, anger, resentment, etc., all the feelings come like a tidal wave to drown me and steal my joy. I'll be the first to admit that I have not mastered this yet. I have to fully rely on God to help me. I've cried tears of anger, tears of frustration, tears of disappointment, but once the crying is over, it's back to reality. The reality of this is bigger than me. If God has called me to it, then He will bring me through it. My actions and decisions may be doing it the hard way, but I'm still learning to trust God with the details. While He is a "big plans for you" God, He's also an "I'm in the details" God. If we look at the details that He gave Noah when the ark was being built and the details of how the temple was to be built and the details of the garments that the priests wore, we can definitely see that He cares about the details. He also cares about the details of my life and yours. He cares about the details of every property I flip, and so do I. I know my contractors get so frustrated with me at times because I expect excellence. The quality of work that goes into the properties we flip is extremely high because that's what I want. Am I over the top? Yes, I am! But I have confidence in knowing that whoever lives in one of my homes will have a quality product. And I can lie down at night knowing it's done right. I expect excellence in workmanship because I do everything as if Jesus were going to live there, and I want to give Him my very best.

Closing Thoughts

I absolutely love being an entrepreneur. It allows me the freedom to spend time with my family, travel, and meet so many wonderful people. It comes with its challenges, of course, but so does life in general. As I have learned (and continue to learn) to walk closer and closer with God and allow the Holy Spirit to live in me and teach me things, I see more and more doors open for me. One of my biggest battles has been fear—fear of failure, fear of being taken advantage of, and fear of lack (a poverty mentality). These are just some of the giants within that I have fought and still fight. Having the mind of Christ is so different from the mindset and limiting beliefs that have been part of my life for oh so many years. Day by day I claim victory by the blood of Jesus! Some days I gain a lot of ground, and some days I lose ground. But I know where my help comes from; it comes from the Lord. I've learned to retreat to a safe place and lay out the plan and ask for new directions. This is such a new way of doing things for me, but it's so much better than my old way of doing things, like falling apart under pressure or freezing up. As I rely more and more on the Holy Spirit to lead me, I find that is where peace is. There's no other place I'd rather be than in His presence, and I will choose that place for the rest of my life.

So make wisdom your quest—
Search for the revelation of
life's meaning.
Don't let what I say go in one
ear and out the other.
Stick with wisdom and she
will stick to you,
Protecting you throughout
your days.
She will rescue all those who
passionately listen to her voice

Proverbs 4:5–6, TPT.

Julie Kresl Richards

Julie Kresl Richards is passionate about seeing people set free and moving forward in their God-given identity empowered and encouraged.

Utilizing her life coach, speaker, teacher, and writer skills, Julie is a consultant to business owners, government leaders, and entrepreneurs—offering personal insight, wisdom, direction, and encouragement. She also trains adults in spiritual direction, freedom, and hearing God for themselves and others.

After seventeen years in the public school system, Julie was at the height of her career as a nationally board-certified teacher, training district staff and positively influencing her school environment as a team leader. One day, she asked God to transition her into another element of her calling: coaching adults and helping them seek greater freedom. That same day, her prayers were answered, and Julie transformed from public educator to professional encourager. Julie has spent seven years working with business leaders and owners through the gift of encouraging prophetic insight known as "Memos From the Head Office," where she has encouraged over 13,000 entrepreneurs.

Currently, Julie functions as a Fractional CEO, or Chief Encouragement Officer, working closely with business owners and influencers to bring their God-sized dreams into reality as well as training others to do the same. Julie also hosts a Facebook membership group called Floating Hope designed specifically for Christians who feel it's time to break free from the limitations holding them back and step into a life filled with renewed hope, purpose, and spiritual empowerment through prophecy and hope.

Find Julie on social media at Julie Kresl Richards or on her website www.juliekreslrichards.com.

Chapter 14

Faith Is the Journey—
Hope Is the Fuel

Would you describe your entrepreneurial adventure as a solution, a sign, or a wonder based on your personal testimony and experience? Explain.

Wonder: a noun—a feeling of surprise mingled with admiration, caused by something beautiful, unexpected, unfamiliar, or inexplicable. (The Oxford Pocket Dictionary, Jul. 2023)

"I can do this. I know I can do this," I mumbled through gritted teeth, tears cascading down my cheeks. I felt silly about the tears, but I couldn't stop them. Frustration had pushed me to the point of anger. My capacity had been reached, and the saddest thing was I couldn't see my way out of it.

My husband of five years and I were living in tight quarters. It was our choice, but that didn't make it easier. We had left the suburbs of Chicago, the place I had lived my whole life, in favor of a wild adventure. We knew there was a place for us with mountains and beautiful blue skies and a vibrant community; we just didn't know how to find it other than this. … We sold our home on the edge of the city, bought a thirty-two-foot travel trailer, and moved in. We hit the road in search of something, somewhere, somehow. All we knew for sure was that God was in it all.

172 | THE JOY-FULL ENTREPRENEUR

As we traveled through thirteen states, we found the majesty of God's creation on Earth complete with the beauty we longed for; however, our forever home was yet to be found, like an itch we couldn't scratch. Exhausted and confused, we paused in San Diego to visit wise friends who advised us to take a much needed pause in our journey. One week of rest stretched into eight months where we moved into thriving, finally discovering what had been missing—community! My husband was welcomed into the worship team at a church we loved while I joined the prophetic prayer team. We both connected with new friends and felt like we had stepped into a warm embrace.

As we settled in this new environment full of opportunities to spread our wings, the tight quarters in our tiny trailer brought moments of frustration. One day, as I cried out to God in annoyance at the trials of moving around in tiny spaces and struggling to make the bed (where I needed to squeeze and crawl and stretch through tears of anger), I heard myself exclaim, "One more foot around the bed … I can't wait for one more foot around the bed!" Miraculously, at that moment, my frustration drained away, and I was filled with hope and excitement for the unseen and unknown. It felt like God stepped into my weariness and created space for me to dream and hope, and I was filled with expectancy. He knew that what was needed was room to expand and grow, and He filled my heart with confidence that it was coming.

This is how God has worked and continues to work in my life and entrepreneurial journey. Surprises create opportunities for me to marvel at the goodness of a God who sees and knows me. He is in the details, big and small.

In that moment of transformation, God gave me renewed hope and capacity. One month later, we moved into a home in what we now know is our Promised Land. God brought us here for a reason, and I am full of wonder about what's next! I know it's going to be good because He is good!

Wonder creates space, making room for God to move. Embracing the many surprises we have in and with God is the best part of the adventure yet!

What Christ-like solutions have you discovered that make your day-to-day business manageable and fruitful?

As I pondered this question and reflected on the remarkable solutions I've discovered, I couldn't help but burst into song, belting out about "my favorite things." I have found this journey to be trial and error, sometimes even trial by fire. In sharing what truly works for me to connect with the Lord in both business and life, I've learned the power of aligning myself with something greater than the world's chaotic ways—a divine alignment with the kingdom of heaven. Grounding myself in timeless wisdom and unloading my burdens daily has become my sanctuary.

When it comes to solutions, it all begins with God. For me, it's about alignment and what or who I choose to align myself with … the world and all its crazy ways or the kingdom of heaven. Making time daily to unload my burdens and to fill myself with timeless, tried-and-true wisdom grounds me.

One practice that has become a lifeline for me I learned from *The Artist's Way: Morning Pages* by Julia Cameron. Every morning, before reaching for my phone or the remote, I grab my journal and my favorite pen. Three pages of stream-of-consciousness writing fills the paper, capturing my thoughts, worries, and all that swirls within me. Then it is time to fill up. Connecting closely with the Lord, I dig into the scriptures, inviting Him into all my broken and vulnerable places with expectancy that He will show up. As I read, inspiration begins flowing, ideas form, and wisdom bubbles up.

Engaging with the Bible often leads me into another cherished practice—two-way journaling or Immanuel Journaling. I learned this method from *Joyful Journey: Listening to Immanuel*, which focuses on developing a mind that mirrors how God thinks about the daily matters of our lives. I find great peace in the first step of the process: Interactive Gratitude. Writing out my thanks to God opens up gates to the presence of God. While gratitude lists are helpful, Interactive Gratitude goes a bit further. It's no longer about us doing all the talking; we pause, wait, and write out

His response. The Lord is always ready to speak; we simply need to learn to attune our ears to hear. Journaling opens up relational pathways to hear from God, and I find it to be invaluable in my day-to-day life!

Last but certainly not least, creating and voicing declarations has been one of my most valuable practices. In my journaling time, certain words or phrases leap off the page, resonating deeply with my thoughts and concerns regarding my business. Some may be words directly from scripture, such as "I can do all things through Christ who strengthens me" (Phil. 4:13, NKJV). Others are crafted phrases that fill me with confidence and empower me to slay the giants of doubt. When I declare these phrases or sentences out loud in various circumstances, my whole countenance shifts as I become aligned with the kingdom of heaven. I walk in confidence, knowing that God knows my business inside and out, backward and forwards, and is guiding me towards the abundant life He has promised (John 10:10b, NKJV).

These practices—Morning Pages, Immanuel Journaling, and declarations—have become my favorite things. They anchor me, connect me with the Divine, and align me with God's promises. And as I continue on this entrepreneurial journey, I cling to these practices as invaluable tools for navigating the complexities of both business and life.

What signs have been given to you along the way that have led you to say yes to exploring and activating your entrepreneurial spirit?

One of my favorite ways that God works in my life is through what I like to call "suddenlies." These sudden events always follow times of prayer, where I've immersed myself in worship, the Word, and praying in pursuit of the presence of God. In my abiding, I find Him. John 15:7 (NKJV) says, "If you abide in Me, and My words abide in you, you will ask what you desire, and it shall be done for you." It is in these times of abiding, where I am living in the felt realization of His presence, that I embrace who He is and what He says, aligning my desires with the kingdom of heaven. Essentially, I take my desires, needs, or wants into a time of pursuing the heart of God, and He transforms my desires into a beautiful representation of His heart for me.

I vividly remember one such "suddenly" moment during my seventeenth year of teaching. Weary of the daily commute, I cried out to God, yearning for a change. Hidden within my heart was a deep desire to leave teaching and pursue more of God through seminary, surrounding myself with those with a heart for God. As I drove through suburban traffic, I poured out my heart to the Lord, every mile covered in tears as I prayed, praised, and worshiped. Upon arriving at school, I eagerly shared my morning commute experience with my office mate and best friend. I recalled that, as I poured out my heart to the Lord on that drive, spending time loving Him, He loved on me. Little did I know that, by the end of the day, a phone call would come, completely blowing my mind and bringing me to my knees in praise. It was an invitation to become the director of a new house of prayer closer to my home. A house of prayer, also known as a "singing seminary," is where worshippers study and sing scripture. God answered my prayer in His unique way, knowing my love for worship and for community. That "suddenly" was the answer to a prayer prayed in the morning with a unique resolution given in the afternoon.

This yes launched me into greater opportunities to serve God and to do so as an entrepreneur, learning how to build and run a business dedicated to the Lord. It was out of that house of prayer that my knowledge of scripture and relationship with the Lord grew exponentially. I learned more about hearing God for myself and others and began teaching adults in spiritual practices to deepen their walk with God—and my coaching business was launched.

Throughout my life, I've come to recognize that sudden answers to prayer are signs of God at work. When opportunity knocks, I have learned to see it as the favor of God. He prepares our hearts for the choices about to be presented, and He gives us the courage to say yes, understanding that none of what we embark upon is a solo journey. When we abide in Him and partner with Him in the process, we walk hand in hand with the

Creator of the universe, navigating the path He has set before us. As I've heard said before, "He gets us ready, and He wastes nothing."

How is "wonder" a part of your rhythm as a leader, visionary, and business builder?

A valuable lesson I learned from a mentor over ten years ago was spoken about his wife and the success of their thirty-plus-year marriage. He said, "Stay in awe." What he meant was to be in daily pursuit of learning new things about your partner. Never assume you know everything there is to know; instead, seek the new. Ask questions. Stay fascinated. Be their greatest admirer and their loudest cheerleader. This nugget of wisdom resonated not only in my marriage but also in my leadership of myself, others, and my business.

I am always learning, constantly evolving. From my early teaching days, I was committed to be a lifelong learner, and that value remains strong in me still. Embracing wonder ignites my curiosity, driving me to seek more knowledge and understanding. It adds fuel to the flame of sitting in the seat of a perpetual learner. There is always more to discover about myself and for myself. As I take risks, try new things, and even stumble and fall, I engage with admiration for how uniquely God designed me for the tasks at hand. Failure doesn't intimidate or deter me; it propels me to try again, embracing a fresh approach.

When I approach others with a heart of wonder, I strive to see them through the eyes of God's love. First John 4:8 (NKJV) says, "Whoever does not love does not know God, because God is love." By connecting with God and seeking Him in the individuals I encounter, whether in business or life, I have the opportunity to speak life and encouragement over them. Then I get to watch as they walk into the fullness of the gold that was revealed in them. Watching the aha moment of revelation, acceptance, and transformation in a person's life never gets old!

The workings of my business never cease to surprise me. By leaning into wonder, I effortlessly transition into a posture of gratitude and praise for every step taken in my work. I wholeheartedly encourage you to embrace wonder as a core value. You will consistently find yourself delighted, mystified, and intrigued by the intricacies of your life.

What does being a joy-full entrepreneur mean to you and how is this emphasized in your daily life?

In life and as an entrepreneur, I have come to understand that I hold the power to set the tone for my life and influence those around me. Our energy, the very essence we carry within, has the ability to shape our atmosphere. I'm sure that you can put your finger on a time when you were having a really good day until you encountered someone who was having a difficult one. This kind of interaction can impact that moment and ripple into the events of the rest of your day. I once faced this challenge head-on when a coworker would visit my classroom each morning to share complaints. Slowly, I began to notice the impact on me spilling onto my students, even after she left. I became short-tempered, nit-picky, and easily frustrated. Sad to say, it took me about a week to recognize what was happening, and I knew I needed to set a boundary. After I explained to my coworker that my top priority was creating a positive and successful day for my students and myself, it made a world of difference, as it fostered an atmosphere of possibility, optimism, and acceptance in my classroom and my work relationships.

For me, *joy* and *happiness* hold distinct meanings. *Happiness* is an emotion that is transient, coming and going. In contrast, *joy* is a state of being. When I immerse myself in the Lord, worshiping and praying, I experience true joy. It is in these moments that I connect to the character and nature of God—a good Father who is never in a bad mood. My joy is rooted in the promises He has made and the anticipation of what lies ahead. I can confidently say that my joy stems from trusting in a faithful God who keeps His word.

As entrepreneurs, we have the power to shape and influence many whom we come into contact with. By choosing to prioritize joy as a state of being, we can create a positive and fulfilling experience that inspires and uplifts ourselves and others.

Who biblically has been a consistent mentor in your pursuit of excellence as an entrepreneur? What are their unique character traits and how have they modeled being a joy-full entrepreneur well?

I love Lydia! She's tucked in the Book of Acts in just a few verses (Acts 16:13–15, 40, NKJV), but her character and openness to follow God speak volumes. What caught my attention initially was her choice of business: luxury purple cloth! I have always adored purple and see it as a beautiful sign of authority and royalty. In a male-dominated Roman Empire, I can imagine her intelligence, perceptiveness, and assertiveness that allowed her to compete and thrive. Lydia was not only highly successful but also open to learning and growth.

When Lydia heard the Word of the Lord spoken through Paul, she responded with obedience, embracing baptism for herself and her household. Her faith was not confined to her personal life; she extended her generosity and hospitality by opening her home for the work of the Lord to continue. In essence, Lydia hosted a house church!

Let's learn from Lydia's story that success in business doesn't mean closing ourselves off from God's leading. She exemplifies the importance of remaining open, embracing opportunities, and seeking God's guidance. Be discerning, assertive, and step out in faith. Create spaces where God's love flourishes. Like Lydia, we can thrive in our entrepreneurial journey with confidence and unwavering faith leading to unspeakable joy.

What has been your biggest challenge or trial in keeping your joy as an entrepreneur and leader?

As an extrovert with a strong focus on service, one of my greatest temptations has been to pour out of an empty cup. To stay in a state of joy, I have found that prioritizing time with the Lord and integrating community into my daily life are essential. In those moments of connection, I allow myself to be reminded of my unique design, identity, and calling to steer clear of the trap of comparison with others.

It's often said that we become the average of the five people we spend the most time with. This significant understanding compels us to carefully choose our circle of influence, and I consistently keep that in mind.

How has your faith been sharpened as an entrepreneur?

Jesus consistently shows up and makes a way. His favor opens doors, and He grants me the courage to walk through them. When I feel limited or inadequate, leaning into Him yields His presence and draws out the best in me. He continually shows me that, when I take a step forward and speak, He completes the sentence. I've learned that trying to do things without Him hasn't served me well in the past. As a team player, I find Jesus to be the best partner ever, supporting and guiding me on this entrepreneurial journey. Never underestimate your influence on the world as you walk hand in hand with Him.

So, fellow dreamers, as you pursue your entrepreneurial goals, remember to never underestimate the impact you can have on the world. Embrace your faith, lean into Jesus, and watch as your influence flourishes beyond your imagination. Open your mouth and allow Him to partner with you in what comes forth. Encouragement fuels the work of the kingdom, and being part of the story is the biggest blessing ever!

Closing Thoughts

My encouragement to you is this: embark on this entrepreneurial journey with faith and hope. Pursue joy, embrace wonder, and lean courageously into your walk with God. In doing so, you'll find yourself on an incredible adventure filled with divine surprises and abundant blessings. Keep pressing on, and remember that God is with you every step of the way. Your entrepreneurial pursuit can make a difference both in your life and the lives of others. Embrace the wonder of the unknown, trust in

God's leading, and step into the joy of making a positive impact on the world. Together, let's shape a better future and leave a legacy of faith and inspiration for generations to come.

I would love to connect with you! Find me on social media at Julie Kresl Richards or on my website at juliekreslrichards.com.

*And we know that in all things
God works for the good of those
who love him, who have been
called according to his purpose*

Romans 8:28.

Tierney Shirrell

Tierney Shirrell is a Christ-follower, wife, mom, and multi-passionate entrepreneur. She started out along the typical Midwest path of college and career, earning her Master's Degree in Accountancy and CPA certification, then moving on to motherhood. Tierney is a former corporate accountant turned full-time mom who found herself in the fight of her life after battling severe postpartum depression and a subsequent diagnosis of bipolar 2 disorder. Through the mental health challenges, she returned to her faith and began to prioritize becoming the Christian woman, wife, mom, friend, mentor, and entrepreneur she knew she was called to be. Tierney discovered solutions that worked for her life and unleashed a desire to help women boldly step into their own unique callings that God placed on their hearts. She developed a framework that helps women overcome their own limitations and become more of who God created them to be one bold step at a time. Tierney is the Founder of the Live BOLD Movement, the prayer-powered personal growth community mentoring women to intentionally live BOLD: (B)rave, (O)bedient, (L)oyal, and (D)etermined with the foundation of Faith and the seven pillars of Family, Freedom, Finances, FARMaceuticals, Fitness, Food, and Fun! She is a podcaster, host of events and retreats, a plant-based wellness advocate, and believer in whole-person well-being—mind, body, soul. When Tierney is not building community and hosting events, she is usually enjoying exploring Arizona with her husband and three kids.

Chapter 15
Journey from Broken to Bold

Would you describe your entrepreneurial adventure as a solution, a sign, or a wonder based on your personal testimony and experience? Explain.

My personal entrepreneurial adventure can be described as a solution due to the isolation, resistance, and limitations that so many of us experience as we step into the callings the Lord places on our hearts and become who He created us to be. It's an ever-evolving process of overcoming and surrender, and I have experienced all of these in my journey from broken to bold.

To really give you an understanding of this journey, I have to take you all the way back to the beginning of my mental health struggles. I can look back now and see God's hand on my life, protecting me and providing the love I so desperately needed. During those years, however, I had turned far away from my faith. Having been raised in religion, but not understanding the need for a personal relationship with the Lord, I didn't become a Christian until high school. When I first accepted Jesus as my Lord and Savior at the age of fourteen, I was on fire in my faith. I was getting into the Word for the first time, reading and studying the Bible, applying it to my life, and deepening my relationship with God.

Unfortunately, I didn't rely on that relationship and faith when my mental health journey began. The deep depression, massive mood swings, and suicidal ideation started in my early college years, beginning a cycle of self-diagnosis, self-medicating, and self-destructive behaviors, which followed me into adulthood, marriage, and motherhood. This all came to a head after the birth of my third baby. I spiraled into severe postpartum depression. And though I'd experienced postpartum following my first two babies, this time was different. I couldn't function or take care of my baby, and I finally reached a breaking point where I believed my family would be better off without me. I found myself sobbing in the shower and mentally composing letters to each of my three children to make sure they'd be ok without me. The thought that I could leave my babies behind scared me enough to finally, after nearly two decades, seek professional help.

I know now that these suicidal thoughts are lies of the enemy, but back then I was trying to do it all in my own strength. At that first appointment when asked why I waited so long to get help, I truthfully answered, "I don't know." As we began to unpack all the symptoms I'd experienced, I realized that my hesitancy to get help was because of a deep need for control and a belief that I had to manage these symptoms myself. I had internalized it as a failure to ask for help. In that very first session, I received a diagnosis of bipolar 2 disorder, and suddenly I felt both the huge burden of managing what I believed to be a lifelong condition and this enormous sense of relief at the same time! All the ups and downs, the rollercoaster of emotions, the ability to successfully function in a six-figure career, and the full-time mom still functioning while hiding this secret darkness—it all finally made sense.

After researching the diagnosis and learning more about brain health issues associated with mental illness conditions, I was angry at God and asking Him why He made me this way. This was just a small step in the direction of my entrepreneurial endeavors, though. God was slowly weaving my pain into purpose and calling me to turn back to Him. Fortunately, my past self-diagnosis cycle had prepared me to be my own advocate in the treatment process. I did my research and knew that, typically, after being diagnosed with bipolar 2 disorder, an individual would be prescribed an initial medication. If that didn't stabilize symptoms, a second medication would be added. If that combination didn't provide the desired results, a third drug was usually prescribed and another after that. This process could continue on until a person was taking a cocktail, on average, of five to six medications. I read countless stories of people who felt worse on all these pharmaceuticals than they did with completely untreated symptoms. I refused to be on multiple prescriptions and thus embarked on one of the most difficult seasons of my life. That first medication made me angry—and not just slightly triggered, but full-on rage and complete emotional instability. Although the recommendation was to add another medication, I insisted on weaning off the first one before beginning a second option. We repeated this process alongside intense therapy, and it took a full year to finally reach a point where I felt emotionally stable.

During this year, parts of me that had been dormant started to wake up again, and little glimpses of my entrepreneurial spirit and strong faith could be seen, but there was still no connection between the two. By this time, my older two kids were in school full-time, and my youngest would soon be starting preschool, so I was feeling like I wanted something for myself. My first venture into entrepreneurship (as an adult) was entering the world of network marketing. I loved the genius business model, but deep down I knew it wasn't going to be my full-time gig. I say first venture "as an adult" because even as a kid, I can see now that the entrepreneurial spirit was part of my makeup. All the way back in middle school, I created a neighborhood kids' club, made flyers and passed them out all over the neighborhood, recruited "employees" from my friends who loved babysitting, and charged a whopping two dollars per kid! After school, I'd gather all the kids together, and we'd provide snacks, crafts, and activities. It's funny to look back at how this was a precursor to my calling as a community builder and founder!

But back to the long and winding journey to get there … dipping my toes into business through network marketing ignited that entrepreneurial spirit within me. And navigating through mental health challenges ignited my faith again. You see, during that really dark season, when I was figuring out how to manage this condition, my husband was handling everything on his own from parenting to financially supporting our family. Thankfully he turned to God. He had a similar background of religion but no relationship, going to church but never really understanding what it actually meant to be a follower of Jesus. I'm so grateful that the Lord worked on my husband's heart and held my family together during this time. God was drawing me back to Him through my marriage and was working things for me to become more of who He had created me to be. The burden my husband felt as the sole provider for our family, along with a whole slew of other factors from his own upbringing (that would be another book in and of itself!), created a lot of fear and limited thinking. As I showed a growing desire to contribute financially to our family and he deepened his own relationship with the Lord, we finally reached a point where he was ready to take a leap of faith and move our family across the country from the Midwest to Arizona, fulfilling a lifelong dream of mine. I had traveled from my tiny northern Illinois town to the beautiful Valley of the Sun as a young child and felt in my soul that I was home. I knew that was where I was meant to live, raise my family, and grow my roots.

(Sidenote: I told my now husband that on the first night we met! But that's a story for another time.)

When we moved to Arizona, we finally found a church home and began to instill Christian values in our family. We also started to work on healing our marriage. I was still a full-time mom with a fun side business, and my husband still had a full-time corporate career while also starting a side gig in network marketing. Both our ventures and my big dreamer mentality were awakening an entrepreneurial spirit in him as well. I began to thrive in the southwest lifestyle. My love of the outdoors, hiking and swimming, and the constant sunshine did wonders for my mental state. I was making healthier nutrition choices, working out regularly, and beginning to think about the possibility of weaning off the one medication I thought I'd be on for the rest of my life. It was at this time that I was introduced to two concepts that would change the trajectory of my journey: plant-based wellness and the world of personal development. Using the combination of plant-based wellness products and my healthy lifestyle, I slowly began to taper down the dosage of the pharmaceutical medication and harness the healing power of God's plants, or as I like to call them, FARMaceuticals. During this time, God was also bringing the personal growth and development industry into my journey, and I connected with a former colleague who was launching her pilot coaching program. When that program ended, I decided to continue working with her as a business coach and invest in a faith coach as well, essentially a Christian-based life coach. Through that business coach, I discovered the network marketing company that aligned with the plant-based wellness that was completely changing my life. Through that faith coach, I was rediscovering my identity in Christ and reestablishing my confidence that comes only from that true identity. I still have that side business helping others with wellness solutions, but, as I mentioned before, I knew there was more to my calling.

During one particular session with my faith coach, I mentioned that my husband and I wanted to start a podcast about relationships being refined through the metaphorical fires, and she said that the name "Mentally Strong Marriage" came to mind. Although we wanted to focus on all relationships, not just marriage, and on more than just the mental wellness journey (which was, of course, one of the many fires my husband and I had faced), I was curious. So I did an internet search of that title and up popped an organization called Mentally Strong. Specifically, it was a video of the founder talking about Mentally Strong coaches, and again my curiosity led me to message the founder asking how one would become a Mentally Strong Coach. She replied that they had previously only trained in-house coaches at their Colorado office location but were piloting an online certification program, and would I be interested? Well, yes, I would! I began the program with seven other trainees and ended up being the only participant to complete it and become a certified Mentally Strong Coach.

I thought I had found my calling and would create my own coaching programs helping people overcome mental health struggles while incorporating plant-based wellness. The best part was that the program had a faith component as well. I had grown so much in my own faith and knew that I couldn't leave that out of the mental wellness journey. But God had bigger plans.

I started using my newly certified skills by volunteering at Phoenix Dream Center, the largest human trafficking recovery program in the United States. Although I'm grateful for the opportunity to serve those women, the horrific things they had experienced were beyond my emotional capacity, and I quickly learned that one-on-one coaching was not where God was calling me. I have a natural tendency to isolate when facing difficulty or mental health struggles, and my spiritual gifts bloomed in a group setting. I didn't know it yet, but God was calling me to create community and to unite women around the common desire to boldly live their own unique callings. I started overcoming the tendency to isolate myself by intentionally taking my thoughts captive and making them obedient to the Word, and I began to pour into other women who were suffering in isolation. I started putting myself in rooms where I was encouraged to be fully me and began to publicly share my story to give others the courage to release the shame and share their stories too. I started gathering women together to talk openly about my own perceived limitations and give them permission to be vulnerable as well. I started small, and God gave me the vision to create a safe space for connection that would grow into the Live BOLD Movement. We are a community of Christ-centered women creating a movement to be BOLD: (B)rave, (O)bedient, (L)oyal, and (D)etermined, to boldly live in God's calling, and to become who He created us to be! My entrepreneurial adventure has created solutions for isolation, resistance, and limitations through community, connection, and prayer-powered personal growth.

What Christ-like solutions have you discovered that make your day-to-day business manageable and fruitful?

As the founder of the Live BOLD Movement, I developed a framework with a foundation of Faith, and the pillars of Family, Freedom, Finances, FARMaceuticals, Fitness, Food, and Fun! These are scripture-based solutions designed to help you live into your calling one bold step at a time. When I initially set out to cultivate community, I was focusing on mental health solutions and was challenged by how to incorporate my faith into my business. Faith was originally one of the pillars in this framework; however, my spirit was convicted when I saw a quote stating, " I made a promise to God that He would be the headline of my business rather than a footnote." I knew that faith had to be the foundation that all the other pillars stood on in order to be effective.

Therefore everyone who hears these words of mine and puts them into practice is like a wise man who built his house on the rock
(Matthew 7:24).

Each of these pillars in life is also tied back to the Word:

- Family: 1 Corinthians 13:4–7
- Freedom: 2 Corinthians 3:17
- Finances: Deuteronomy 10:14
- FARMaceuticals: Ezekiel 47:12
- Fitness: 1 Corinthians 6:19–20
- Food: 1 Corinthians 10:31
- Fun: Ecclesiastes 3:12

I have discovered that focusing on and applying these verses in business and life are the solutions to make both manageable and fruitful.

What signs have been given to you along the way that have led you to say yes to exploring and activating your entrepreneurial spirit?

The biggest sign God has given to me along the way is that the same verse seems to pop up everywhere—in songs, sermons, conversations, podcasts, etc. That verse is found in the book of Romans. "And we know that in all things God works for the good of those who love him, who have been called according to his purpose" (Romans 8:28). I use "8:28" as a verb meaning God can 8:28 anything—He wastes nothing, no pain, no mistake, no suffering. If we let God direct our path, whatever we've walked through is something He can use to bless someone else's life. This verse has been so significant in activating my entrepreneurial spirit and saying yes to my calling that I got it tattooed on my left wrist. It serves as a daily reminder that God will use all the brokenness, working everything for good for a purpose to serve others.

How has your faith been sharpened as an entrepreneur?

As an entrepreneur, my faith has been sharpened by the people in my communities. One of my most influential mentors taught me that there are three crucial communities you need in your entrepreneurial journey: one of people further along that can mentor you, one of people in similar stages that can collaborate with you, and one of people you can pour into. I've intentionally surrounded myself with people in each of these types of communities in order to grow my faith and help others grow theirs.

How do you market your business and faith? What is your belief system in showcasing one over the other and how have you come to peace with your personal solution?

I used to joke that events were my love language. I now understand it is one of my spiritual gifts. I love hosting and creating an experience for everyone in attendance, from holding a dinner party with a few friends, to leading a full-day retreat for hundreds of women ... and anything in between. When I first felt the call to create a community, I struggled with how to incorporate my faith. Even though I loved hosting events for my network marketing business, I didn't yet understand the connection of plant-based wellness with faith. I never seemed to gain any traction in building a team with that business because I wasn't fully in alignment with my calling. I began cultivating community in the mental health space online, but knew, once again, that this wasn't the direction God was leading me. I knew that I craved real connection in person with like-minded and like-hearted women, and through attending personal development events, my calling became clearer and activated. I loved the personal growth space, but I felt God telling me that He needed to be at the center of that journey. I began to see the vision of combining my love for hosting events with my love for personal growth, all centered on love for the Lord. God began to place people in my life who inspired me to take action on that vision; however, I still had fear and lingering doubt. I was known for talking about plant-based wellness and mental health. Who was I to now start talking about living into God's calling? But God, once again, brought the right people and mentors who shared a similar vision to serve women not just in business but in whatever calling God had placed on their hearts. This shift gave me such peace because I was finally walking in full alignment with my personal calling. I now boldly market my business as prayer-powered personal growth, cultivating Christ-centered connection and sharing the gifts God has given me through the hosting of those events that I love so much.

Closing Thoughts

The joy-full entrepreneurial journey has been one of self-discovery, ups and downs, twists and turns, sometimes holding on for dear life, terrifying and full of uncertainty, all while being the beautiful fulfillment of my God-given calling. I'm called to be the light in the personal growth industry that so often leaves faith out. I'm called to build community, cultivate a safe space for both vulnerability and big dreams, and activate a movement of women boldly living in God's calling. To become part of this movement, join our membership community at liveboldmovement. com and connect through our podcast Live BOLD Movement.

*A man's gift makes room
for him and brings him
before great men*

Proverbs 18:16.

Tamika Thomas

Tamika is a tenacious woman who has faced numerous challenges throughout her life but has never given up. She is a devoted mother and wife and has also made a name for herself as a successful podcaster, CEO of Tuesday with Tamika, coach, consultant and author. With six published books under her belt, she has become an inspiration to many with her words of encouragement and guidance. Despite the obstacles she has faced, Tamika remains an embodiment of strength and resilience and continues to inspire others to overcome their own struggles. She fully lives and embodies her tagline "live a life to inspire and not impress."

Chapter 16
Heal, Deal, and Build God's Way

Would you describe your entrepreneurial adventure as a solution, a sign, or a wonder based on your personal testimony and experience? Explain.

I wonder if she'll ever be able to read and write? I wonder if she'll ever be caught up to her actual grade? I wonder how they let her get this far behind? This is what people used to wonder about me, and rightfully so. I was two grades behind and was unable to even write or spell my name at eight years old. So their whispers and wonders were not because they were mean or judgmental; they were honest and worried. But God has always been holding the pen, and He was going to have a "watch this" moment through my story.

Growing up as the oldest child of a sixteen-year-old mother who was addicted to drugs and alcohol, people whispered and wondered if I would ever be successful. I grew up in a gang-infested home and experienced tragedy after tragedy from the age of zero to seven. I remember being labeled a "bad kid." I didn't understand it then, but I understand now that kids would rather be labeled "bad" than "dumb." Also living in our three-bedroom house were my five younger siblings, my grandmother, my aunt and her two kids, and two uncles, one of whom was murdered due to gang violence. At seven I was removed (or rescued, I should say) from my mother's home. Thankfully, I was placed in the custody of my father after being hit and nearly killed by a car.

When I arrived at the unfamiliar home of my dad, stepmom, and two younger siblings, I was embarrassed by the fact that I knew how to do a lot of things, like steal, fight, and manipulate, but reading and writing weren't on my list of things I could do. I'll never forget how I felt as a little girl listening to my new teacher tell my dad, "She's so far behind, I'm not sure we will be able to help her, but if she works hard, she will catch up." I often imagine God up in heaven laughing when people place limits on His children. I imagine Him sitting high and looking low thinking, "Keep watching; I am about to work a miracle."

My dad, being a man of faith, prayed after he met with my new teachers and sat me in front of a simple book, which started my process of learning and re-learning. After that book, the first book I remember being able to read all the way through was *If you Give a Mouse a Cookie* by Laura Numeroff. I didn't know it then, but God was working a wonder in me. Jeremiah 29:11(NKJV) tells us: "For I know the plans and thoughts that I have for you declares the Lord." My life has been filled with every type of abuse you can think of. Witnessing my mom go in and out of jail, surviving drive-by shootings at our home, and being labeled the dumb kid were all part of God's plan for me to be a wonder for the world to see. Even today, I struggle and often wonder why God has chosen me. I have become like that little mouse in the book. I am persistent in my business helping women heal, just like God has healed me. Daily, I sit in wonderment and in awe of how God blesses me over and over again. And I am blessed to now hear people whisper, "Wow, she has been through all that, and look at her now." My life and entrepreneurial adventure have truly been a wonder of God's grace, love, and purpose for the lives of those that the world would label broken. God has shown me and others through my testimony that He alone can turn our trials into treasures; I *wonder* if you would trust Him to do the same for you.

What Christ-like solutions have you discovered that make your day-to-day business manageable and fruitful?

Did you know that the Bible mentions rest over fifty-seven times in the New Testament? Luke 5:16 tells us that Jesus often withdrew to a lonely place and prayed. When I think of what Christ-like solutions I use in my day-to-day business to make it manageable and fruitful, I can't help but to think it includes resting, retreating, and being open to receive just as Jesus did. There are moments, like during a big launch, writing a book, or a big marketing campaign, that I feel like I'm going one million miles per hour and surviving off of caffeine and very little sleep. But once it's all over and the water settles, I literally have learned to rest. I believe that this is such a Christ-like solution that many entrepreneurs miss because the world teaches us to grind and that sleep is for the weak. But if we are modeling our life and business after Christ, we know the importance of rest. Even when going through difficult times, when my business is not yielding the results I planned for, I have learned to rest. Isaiah 30:15 is another great reminder of what happens when we rest and receive. The people of Israel were complaining after putting their trust in Egypt's protection instead of in God. Many times God will take us out of our personal Egypt, and we will complain to everyone instead of resting in the promises of God. I've learned that complaining literally blocks blessings, so I choose to rest and receive just as Christ did.

What signs have been given to you along the way that have led you to say yes to exploring and activating your entrepreneurial spirit?

God is amazing at giving us signs, and often it is through the most common everyday things. I'll never forget God giving me a sign as I was traveling to a speaking engagement. My destination was in the mountains in a very high and secluded area. As I drove higher into the mountains, I lost Internet connection, which ultimately caused me to lose my GPS service. Panicking, I turned all the way around and returned to a spot where

I was able to reconnect to the Internet. I studied the directions and was confident that I could successfully make it back up the mountain. When I arrived at my location, I realized that I had been literally one street away before I turned around. Unfortunately, turning around caused me to lose valuable time. I believe that this was a sign for me to keep going on my entrepreneurial journey and to not turn around and start over. The higher we go, it's very possible that we will lose connection, or we won't get the validation that we're going in the right direction. But God always gives us a sign that we're "one street away" and to keep pursuing the entrepreneurial spirit.

How do you allow supernatural signs to direct your path, process, profit plan, and partnerships in business?

As a faith-based entrepreneur, allowing supernatural signs to direct my path, process, profit plan, and decisions concerning those I partner with has literally been a cornerstone of my business. I've heard the cliché many times from other kingdom entrepreneurs that God is their CEO. I've taken it a step further and have daily business meetings, a.k.a. prayer, with my CEO. Funny thing is, He doesn't have standard operating hours. He tends to call me for business meetings between the hours of two and three a.m. One morning during a "business meeting," He told me He wanted to show me something. I went into an open vision of eight-year-old me at a school assembly. This vision was so real that I felt like I was actually there. I remember eight-year-old me sitting perfectly, hoping that I would get called on by the presenter of the assembly, when suddenly, all of the other students disappeared, and God appeared on the stage. He laughed and played and danced with me, and then right before the assembly ended, He spoke. He told me in order for me to be successful, in order for me to have a profitable business and attract aligned partnerships, I had to let go of perfectionism, pretending, and performing. Interestingly enough, eight-year-old me, if you remember, was the version of me that struggled with reading and writing. I did not realize that, before this supernatural sign, I had been running businesses through the lens of perfectionism, pretending, and performing because I was still trying to prove that I was smart enough to run a business. God showed me at that early morning business meeting that, in order to have a true kingdom business, I had to let go of those things and allow Him to direct my path through authenticity and transparency.

Who biblically has been a consistent mentor in your pursuit of excellence as an entrepreneur? What are their unique character traits and how have they modeled being a joy-full entrepreneur well?

The Proverbs 31 woman has been a consistent mentor in my pursuit of excellence as an entrepreneur. She has five unique character traits that I have modeled on how to be a joyful entrepreneur. I will break down those five traits and show you how you can implement them into your business.

1. She **served** God with all of her heart, mind, and soul and sought His will for her life (Prov. 31:26). Keep God the head of your life. Constantly seek Him. Never make your business an idol, understanding that it's a gift that God has given you.
2. She was a **trustworthy** helpmate (Prov. 31:11). Trustworthy is synonymous with having integrity. God will bring business deals, clients, income, and influence when He knows He can trust us. Work with integrity.
3. She was a **loving** mother and taught her children the ways of the Father (Prov. 31:28). Our family is our first ministry. Learn how to harmonize family and business. When we do right by our family, who God has entrusted us to minister to, He can broaden our reach and give us people to serve in our business
4. She was a **good steward** of her gifts and spent her money wisely (Prov. 31:16). Stewarding our gifts is huge. One of my favorite influencers, Patrice Washington, says, "Give God something to

bless." When you live by that motto, you will steward your gifts well.

5. She was **diligent** and completed her daily tasks (Prov. 31:19). Daily, write a list of non-negotiables. Do your best to complete all your non-negotiables so you can rest and receive.

What has been your biggest challenge or trial in keeping your joy as an entrepreneur and leader?

My biggest challenge and trial in keeping my joy as an entrepreneur and leader has been the process of healing and building. God revealed to me that I could only build to the level that I was willing to heal. But healing is painful. Healing can be slow. And sometimes healing causes us to isolate. But I understand that, in order for me to build the business that I pray about, I have to be willing to heal the parts of me I have been so comfortable hiding behind. Healing is a seed that reaps joy. It is watered in tears and comfortability. And when the garden of pain is properly tended to, the harvest of joy is abundant.

I want to leave you with the process I use to heal and build.

Step one: Be honest, and acknowledge the pain from your past.

Step two: Don't do the work alone. Find a community that loves and supports you.

Step three: Turn the trial into a treasure. This is how we find the joy to continue on the journey.

Closing Thoughts

It has truly been a joy sharing my joyful entrepreneur journey with you. Through this journey, I believe God has been with me every step of the way saying, "Watch this." I pray that you are blessed by knowing you are a wonder of God, and all of the scars that you have acquired in your life are truly for the making of you. I hope that you remember to rest and receive all the great things that God has in store for you. It is imperative to let go of perfectionism, pretending, and performing! Your audience is waiting for the true and authentic version of you. Follow the blueprint of the Proverbs 31 woman. She is truly a joyful entrepreneur. And lastly, release the need to hide behind what you need to heal. It's time to build men and women of God. I would love for you to continue this journey of joyful entrepreneurship and healing with me on my weekly podcast *Tuesday with Tamika* streamed everywhere you listen to podcasts. Let's also connect on social media. I would love to be a part of your tribe, and I want to welcome you into mine, where we believe in lifting as we climb, turning our trials into treasures, living a life to inspire and not impress, and allowing God to fully restore us. Love you!!! Oh, and don't forget to journal. Grab your journal and title a page "Watch This." Record all the ways God has proven that you are a wonder of His grace and mercy. The process will blow your mind.

Behold, I am doing a new thing; now it springs forth, do you not perceive it? I will make a way in the wilderness and rivers in the desert

Isaiah 43:19.

Anthony Hart

I am just a real dude who is blessed to be called boo, daddy, pastor, veteran, podcaster, and pioneer. These are not titles but terms of endearment and positioning moments in my life to seek out my God-given purpose: Boo to the amazing, talented, driven, and beautiful Morgan Hart. Daddy to one humble, intelligent son and two patience-cultivating daughters. Pastor at Greenbrier Community Church in Chesapeake, VA (goGCC.org), with a Bachelor's of Science in Christian Leadership and Management from Regent University. Veteran of the United States Navy after 21 years of service as a Chief Petty Officer trained to oversee and operate aircraft carrier nuclear reactors. Voice of the *In the Red* podcast that is seeking to bring fresh perspectives through stories of people who don't look like you, act like you, or sound like you. (This is that uncomfortable place where we are challenged, and we can truly see that we are stronger together than apart.) Pioneer who pursues taking the message of Jesus out of the confines of an inanimate church building and into every area of life through the intimate connection with believers and their testimonies. Fellow Founder and Pastor of The Founder Collective—a mobilized church for visionary leaders.

Afterword:
Activation—Power of Response

When I was initially asked to be a part of this anthology, it was in the form of writing a foreword, which I would have said yes to. Being an author for the first anthology, strongly believing in the content presented, and knowing most of the authors, I would have had all that I needed to invite you to dive into this book headlong. Through the process of developing this anthology, however, I was moved from the front of the bus to the back. Or in my own terms, I went from the capital letter at the beginning of the sentence to the exclamation point at the end. This shift intrigued and challenged me because of the difference in content and context required.

Forewords are aimed at inviting you into the book, connecting you with its authors, and praising the content displayed through their writings. These are meant to get your attention but are quickly forgotten, and rightfully so, once the meat of the book is accessed. A conclusion is a whole other ball game. I saw it more closely connected with a response to the material. For an anthology, this can be a daunting task because of the multitude of data and perspectives provided from the many authors. How do I bridge the gap between their differing stories and their individual connection to solutions, signs, and wonders promised by the title of the book? How do I sum up all of these amazing testimonies of growth? How do I add anything without taking something away? Are you as overwhelmed as I felt? (I forgot to tell you that I am an overthinker.) Then it clicked. My task is to connect with the one consistent variable throughout every word, page, and chapter of this book … you.

I hope I have your attention because I want to ask you two questions that I do not feel we ask enough. The first is "Why are you here?" Something caused you to pick this book up. Maybe it was a connection to one of the authors, or perhaps the title caught your attention. No matter why, there is purpose in you reading this book. As a pastor, I realize that God is in the most minute of details, and when He wants to get your attention, He will. So whether you grabbed this book because you were looking for solutions to connecting your faith and business or merely intrigued by the signs and wonders tagline, there was purpose in this time spent with these authors and their stories.

Now that we have established you are here for a reason, the second question is "What do you do with this data and experience? Were you stretched by the perspectives shared and enlightened through the personally lived stories? Were you challenged to evaluate your own business, family, and life through the lens of these authors? Or, as in my case, did this merely validate the journey you have been on and helped you to realize that you are not the only one trying to figure this out?

Whether you know it or not, you have had or will have a response to the information gathered in this anthology. There will be an effect on you based on your own story and how it compares to theirs. The power of response is realizing what you are responding to. If we move with intent, it will either be away from something or towards something. Think about that for a minute. Look over your life, successes and defeats, and ask yourself were they in response to merely running from something or was there an intentional movement towards a goal or a better place.

In conversations with people in business across the spectrum of what many would deem "success," I find this question to be one of the most revealing about peace and joy in their business, home, and life. Many who have run from broken situations, like abusive parents, broken homes, or merely a desire to be better than where they came from, constantly find themselves struggling to be satisfied or to find a place of purpose. This mindset can cause two major issues:

1. Looking over your shoulder prevents you from focusing on what lies ahead.
2. Comparing where you are to a broken past can provide very limited goals. It is not hard to be better than your worst, but is that where you want to be?

Now you may be asking, what does this have to do with my faith. My answer to you would be that Jesus' whole purpose was to remove your need to run from things so that you could focus on running to Him. From His disciples to broken people, like the adulteress, Jesus constantly used words like *come* and *go* to demonstrate a required shift in our paths. In the case of the disciples, it was a group of men who had been told that they were not smart enough or good enough to be religious leaders. Jesus' invitation to them was to leave behind the known of their capabilities and follow Him into the unknown of their availability (John 1:43). Their focus was required to shift from being invaluable to a pursuit of the most valuable.

In the example of the adulteress, Jesus found her in her lowest moment possible. Caught in the act of a crime punishable by death, He removed the noise of her accusers and gave her an option. She could stay stuck on a path to death based on the shame and disappointment of a life in response to brokenness. Maybe it was a cycle of broken relationships that left her constantly seeking healing from people who were broken just like her, or perhaps it was a response to not receiving love and attention from loved ones that drove her to look for it anyplace she could find it. Regardless of how she got there, Jesus gave her a new option. He removed the condemnation and said, "go, and from now on sin no more" (John 8:11, ESV). Her focus was required to shift from ending to just beginning.

So now I circle back around to you and ask, where do you go from here? But I must warn you. This shift in focus is not always the easiest or most comfortable. It may differ from those around you who were ok with you being stuck running from things because it validated their ability to do the same. The good news is that there is always someone who has gone before you. Maybe their journey hasn't looked identical to yours, but they had to make the same decision as you—to change what you are responding to and how you are responding to it.

Solutions, signs, and wonders is merely an invitation to seek something that lies ahead of you. In the words of the Apostle Paul, people "should seek God, and perhaps feel their way toward him and find him. Yet He is actually not far from each one of us" (Acts 17:27, ESV). This is an invitation to allow God access into all areas of your life: areas of hurt so that you can be healed, your business so that you can find direction and be a blessing to the world around you, and your family so that you can find peace and connection in the place meant to recharge you. None of these authors got there overnight or even arrived at someplace of completion. They are all walking out the same journey you are on. Along the way, they just had to make the decision to start walking towards something.

I leave you with this prayer.

Dear Heavenly Father, we are so thankful for your faithfulness and that you value us beyond what we can see or imagine. I pray that our desire would be to blindly feel as we seek you, knowing full well that we will find you (Acts 17:27). Let our hearts be in constant pursuit of you so that we can carry your love, grace, and mercy in all areas of our lives. I pray that you would open our eyes to our purpose and the provision that accompanies it as we follow you. In Jesus' name, Amen.

What are you still doing here? **It is time to GO**.

the joyfull

E N T R E P R E N E U R

Are you already operating as a Joy-full Entrepreneur and want to partake in our next compilation project?

Or perhaps you want to take a deeper dive.. Get a hold of the first book in our series where we unpacked principles, power and presence!

F.I.T. in FAITH
PRESS

1 CHRONICLES 16:24 (NLT)

Publish his glorious deeds among the nations.
Tell everyone about the amazing things he does.

A Christian Publishing House dedicated to bringing the stories of founders, innovators and trailblazers to life. Encompassing a shared mission with F.I.T. in Faith Media, the emphasis on obliterating shame and activating purpose opens conversations around mental, physical, relational, financial and spiritual health and wholeness journeys, often directly associated to their rooted identity and purpose driven life.

Learn More
&
Don't Wait to Get
Published!

JOIN THE
F.I.T. in Faith Network Resource Hub!

IT'S TIME TO ACTIVATE YOUR *god dream*

DOWNLOAD NOW!

The F.I.T. in Faith Network Resource Hub will serve as a growth tool for you as a Joy-full Faith-fueled Entrepreneur.

SPEAK, WRITE, BUILD, TESTIFY

Count this app as your Aaron and Hurr on your fulfilling and sometimes hard days of blazing the trail of your purpose-driven calling.

- SOUND BIBLICAL BUSINESS SUPPORT - COURSES & CONTENT
- TRAINING & IMPLEMENTATION TOOLS
- TEMPLATES
- QUICK START RESOURCES
- FINANCIAL TRAJECTORY PLANS & MODELS
- COMMUNITY CONNECTIONS - FOCUS GROUPS
- LIVE OFFICE HOURS MONTHLY WITH Q&A AND ON THE SPOT COACHING

let's find out your

PROFIT INDENITY

Reveal Your Passion and Spiritual Gifts
Connection to Start & Grow Your Business

TAKE THE QUIZ TODAY!

Have you ever wondered what your purpose is?

Or how you could use your gifting as an entrepreneur?

Or, perhaps, how your spiritual gifts are connected to your prosperity?

Or how your passion propels your profit?

founder
COLLECTIVE

This is a movement of empowered founders liberating others to stand in freedom, firm in their identity, activating authority as Kingdom citizens.

WE ARE THE MOBILIZED CHURCH!

A free ebook edition
is available with the
purchase of this book.

To claim your free ebook edition:

1. Visit MorganJamesBOGO.com
2. Sign your name CLEARLY in the space
3. Complete the form and submit a photo of the entire copyright page
4. You or your friend can download the ebook to your preferred device

Morgan James
BOGO™

A **FREE** ebook edition is available for you
or a friend with the purchase of this print book.

CLEARLY SIGN YOUR NAME ABOVE

Instructions to claim your free ebook edition:
1. Visit MorganJamesBOGO.com
2. Sign your name CLEARLY in the space above
3. Complete the form and submit a photo of this entire page
4. You or your friend can download the ebook to your preferred device

Print & Digital Together Forever.

Snap a photo

Free ebook

Read anywhere

Printed in the USA
CPSIA information can be obtained
at www.ICGtesting.com
JSHW082107120424
61084JS00002B/46

9 781636 982946